Narco Night Train

A Dissident View of the American Narcostate

A Harm City Book

Dust Cover
In *Narco Night Train* counterculture urban violence writer James LaFond offers a selection of stranger than fiction truths to illustrate the massive threat to personal autonomy that is the 21st Century American Narco State. You do not have to agree with the author that the people of America are being drugged into insensibility and led up the chronologic meat chute to agree that drug use and The Drug War in the United States are cultural driving mechanisms.

Unlike other authors who write on this subject LaFond, a 'Darwinist', offers no social solutions to the problems he cites. One gets the idea that he would prefer this insanity to continue so that he will never be short of writing material. *Narco Night Train* is simply a heads up that your world is chugging to a very real Hell on the rails that your granddaddy laid with high hopes.

All aboard!

Books by James LaFond

Nonfiction

The Fighting Edge, 2000
The Logic of Steel, 2001
The First Boxers, 2011
The Gods of Boxing, 2011
All Power Fighting, 2011
When You're Food, 2011
The Lesser Angles of Our Nature, 2012
The Logic of Force, 2012
The Greatest Boxer, 2012
Take Me to Your Breeder, 2014
The Streets Have Eyes, 2014
Panhandler Nation, 2014
The Ghetto Grocer, 2014
American Fist, 2014
Don't Get Boned, 2014
Alienation Nation, 2014
In The Chinks of The Machine, 2014
How the Ghetto Got My Soul, 2014
Saving the World Sucks, 2014
Taboo You, 2014
The Fighting Life, 2014
Narco Night Train, 2014
Into the Mountains of Madness, 2014

Fiction

Astride the Chariot of Night, 2014
Sacrifix, 2014

Rise, 2014
Motherworld, 2014
Planet Buzzkill, 2014
Fruit of The Deciever, 2014
Forty Hands of Night, 2014
Black and Pale, 2014
Daughters of Moros, 2014
Fat Girl, 2014
Hurt Stoker, 2014
Poet, 2014
Triumph, 2015
Winter, 2015
The Spiral Case, 2015
Hemavore, with Dominick Mattero, 2015
Yusuf of the Dusk, 2015
Mantid, 2015
RetroGenesis: Day 1, with Erique Watson, 2015

Sunset Saga Novels

Big Water Blood Song, 2011
Ghosts of the Sunset World, 2011
Beyond the Ember Star, 2012
Comes the Six Winter Night, 2012
Thunder-Boy, 2012
The World is Our Widow, 2013
Behind the Sunset Veil, 2013
Den of The Ender, 2013
God's Picture Maker, 2014
Out of Time, 2015
Seven Moons Deep, 2015

For Machete Ricardo, may you find your freedom
home, and The Sensibles, may you keep yours

Contents

Narco State Anatomy
Preface to the Owner's Manual for Your Ankle-
strapped Handgrips

I am not a conspiracy theorist. I do, however,
regard organizations as social organisms, living
things that, like humans, have a conscious process,
and a subconscious drive to survive, which, when
successful, morphs into a drive to thrive. The
individual components of a thriving organization
tend to make many decisions and take many
actions which result in the strengthening of that
social organism. Do you, for instance, think about
breathing?

Perhaps the most salient metaphor for this
'subconscious political will' is team sports, most
notably football of the American variety.

The average idiot sees a company, a polity, or a
military formation as a top down expression of one
person's autocratic will. The entire reason for the
sham presidential elections every four years is the
reinforcement of this peasant mentality to see the
great lord in his great house as the fount of all
things good and ill. In it modern form, one might
actually equate the second term of a modern
president to the ancient practice of assigning a
scapegoat to take the blame for a community's
misfortune.

To better understand the living nature of social organisms the football team makes for a nice example, for it is such an organism, if only intended as a diversion for the brutish masses so that they might not come to understand the activities of their masters for what they are. The football team further makes an ideal example for a thriving and striving social organism because its workings are grossly apparent. Where much of the running of a baseball team is done by obscured men crouching gnome like in their dens, the football coaching staff is almost entirely visible, as are the support staff and the various squads of players at rest and play, all visible simultaneously.

Any look at a football team—on the field and on the sideline—will reveal a complex multifaceted social organism focused on a number of very obvious tasks. The game will reveal the head coach as merely one of perhaps a hundred moving parts in a machine whose every gear seems to have the opportunity for–at least temporarily—autonomous action. And, like the law of unintended consequences cited by libertarian thinkers when discussing social engineering, one can never predict the exact outcome of a football play.

Keeping in mind the inertia and unpredictable consequences of the actions of social organisms, let's enumerate the basic equation whereby the illicit drug economy has become the social driver in the postmodern world.

1. Rich politicians take working class and middle class money to pay poor women to avoid marriage and spawn armies of feral youths, thereby guaranteeing cultural decay, rendering the population ripe for stage 3.
2. That welfare money gushes up the economic latter to superrich corporations by many and diverse ways.
3. The purposeless poor, idle rich, despondent working class, and shrinking middle class turn to drugs to deaden the pain of this inauthentic existence. As I write most Americans are either legally or illegally medicated against pain, stress, depression, anxiety, or—my favorite—addiction!
4. The rich politicians criminalize drugs, accelerating the suction of money from the ghetto to the penthouse and simultaneously the growth of the state at the expense of the middle class and working class.
5. The resulting Narco State, built on the sham drug war and the booming drug trade, wages continuous external war and warns of a coming internal war against terrorists.
6. The Narco State is, by means I do not fully understand, here, apparently to stay, and so long as it fails to win the drug war that it wages, will continue to thrive.
7. Just as victory in the internal drug war would emasculate the Narco State, victory over, or peace with, the external Islamist forces could expose the drug war for the sham it is—so

the Manhattan versus Mecca proxy war most
not be fought to a conclusion or abandoned.

Hos Yos and Mo-fos

This week, on three occasions I have walked by the local bank ATM as a group of youthful black muggers stood like sentinels around it. A group of adult men drinking malt liquor and minding their own business on a secondary street corner would be rousted by the cops. But these predators are ignored by the cops like lions avoid jackals; two sets of unequally matched predators, one hunting the other scavenging and hunting lesser prey.

I have seen the cops arrest or stop three middle aged white men in this same time period. The muggers and the cops are preying on the same animal, the middle aged stoner or alcoholic, consigned to a life on foot in one of America's most dangerous cities.

This Sunday morning I was out walking down my street when a hooker approached me from behind. I crossed the street and she sped up and followed, asking for a cigarette. I nodded 'no' and ignored her but she came closer and shadowed me like a half naked slave girl living under Sharia law. I was glaring around, ignoring her, looking for the man or men who might be her accomplice in my robbery. I was visualizing hammer fisting her teeth down her throat before I grabbed her and threw at the legs of her buck, then she broke my slide into psychopathy with her prematurely gravel-tone voice, "Excuse me. Can I walk with you t the main road? Please sir, you like you can take care of you. Two males—young black ones—have been robbing women on this street, all the way back to Belair Road. You should let your women you know about it. I wouldn't want it to happen to them."

I remained silent, but permitted the whore to walk off my right shoulder. When we got to Harford road she ran for it, like some English woman running for the subway when the air raid sirens went off during the Battle of Britain.

That was just another Sunday morning in the Narcostate, a world crafted into a twisted corpse of a nation by our masters in their ceaseless war on self-medication. To my dissident mind the war on drugs is a scheme to drug the population and at the same time build a massive police state.

It is what it is. The best I can hope for is to survive for a while in its writhing ruin and leave a record for some member of a hopefully sane world that might rise from the haze of this one when it finally implodes.

-James LaFond, Friday, 10/24/2012

That Guy: With the Book!

Intellectual Speed Bump for the Next Revolution?

This past weekend I found myself in a mixed-age rap sessions. Six young men and three of us older guys were engaged in a wide ranging conversation about music, guns, civilization, the government as techno mom, and censorship. I kept quiet, letting one of the other old men answer most of the youthful queries. I was surprised at how many of these youths and twenty-somethings were deeply concerned about the latest revelations of Federale spying on U.S. citizens. Only one of them had read Orwell's 1984, so there were not a lot of literary reference points to be dredged up. There was though, a creeping sense that the government was coming for them, to take away whatever freedom they might have.

I stayed in the shadows of the conversation, but was continually drawn in as a fact verifier and sounding board. I did describe what precautions I had taken in wording my articles in such a way as to minimize search engine results that might bring me to light as a literary dissident. I don't think my sword and shield will do much to save me from a squad of Homeland Security goons, and I certainly do not want to be Commander Booty Master's cellmate. [See Black Gorilla Family News #1] I did nod in agreement to most of my military friend's assertions about Federale intentions and the fragile and transitory nature of personal and local autonomy.

I see a corporate police state in the making; a Rollerball [the 1970s James Conn movie] type of future where a handful of fat-cats milk us like cows to pad their luxurious life. My quest is little enough; just the pursuit of a free opinion and the ability to walk to and from my destination free of physical attack and law enforcement harassment.

But the minds present were both old and defiant and young and idealistic. Eventually, as one of the youths admitted to his plans to form an armed gang to combat Federale storm troopers when they rolled into his neighborhood to impose martial law, another asked the military man, how long they had to prepare; what would be the tripwire sign that the Federale Hounds of War were being loosed on him and his?

As the most passive participant in this conversation, the one that insisted on not picking sides for or against the evil Federales, I was shocked at the former paratrooper's verdict. "You want to know when they're coming to get you, to take your guns, to requisition your vehicle?"

He then stepped behind me and put his hands lovingly on my shoulders. "Keep an eye on this man. He is an intellectual—a self-educated and published author; a dissident—when they drag him out of his house and throw a jacket over his head, you will never see him or any other independent voice again. He will be silenced, and you're next, without him and his kind there to tell you it is coming."

I feigned insult, and said, "Why me?"

He then pointed to the other retired military man for verification, the elder one, who saw combat in Indochina when I was a baby. The old veteran made a pistol out of his thumb and finger, pointed it at me, and said, "Back in Cambodia—you know, that country we were never in, fighting the Chinese that were never there—my CO would have pointed at him and said, 'Shoot his ass!' and pop, I would have done it."

Thanks guys. I better hurry up and finish writing that history book. My getting snuffed would be a cool postscript.

Narco Night Train

A Night Roasting in the Flaming Cultural Wreckage We Are Riding to Hell [You are not allowed to read this Mom.]

I would like the general reader to gain some insight into this nation's burgeoning drug culture. This article concerns primarily my experiences of the night of Monday, August 12, 2013 into the early morning hours of the 13th. It is firmly in the vein of my Narco-state News pieces. It is, however, modeled on—and may be regarded as a sequel to— Harm City Holdout, an article I did early last winter, concerning another insane trip through Baltimore City by night.

Midnight in the Narcostate [1:35 AM 8/8/13]

I waited in line to purchase my beverage at the food market where I am employed as a night clerk. I stood behind a mated pair of whitetrashians [perhaps the two that a later day Noah might take off in his Ark to reseed the post-delluvian world with drug addicts] who were having a hard time getting their transaction to go through. They had two 'food stamp' or EBT cards, on this, the second day of distribution. Both cards had insufficient funds. These cards are recharged with between $30 and $1,800 per month, so I assume they had not yet gotten their various infusions of government largess.

The bill was $26.32. What then occurred has often occurred while I was manning the checkout; the male of the pair pulled out a knot-roll of twenties so thick it barely fit in his pocket, peeled off two, made the purchase, and left.

The cashier was bemused, and, after they left, looked at me and said, "What the fuck?"

Another customer chimed in, "He sells pills. I know him from back in the neighborhood. You don't make money on weed anymore. Everybody is a junky on pills in this neighborhood."

A Stoner, Zombie Skank Sighting [9:27 AM 8/8/13]

Late that morning, tired from my shift working frozen food, I walked a little over a mile to a bus stop. I stood off by fifty yards as all of these bus stop patrons use the two lines I use to get to hospital and community center drug treatment programs. They are still practicing addicts though:

taking methadone, smoking vast quantities of cigarettes, and eating as many prescription pain pills and antipsychotics as they can get their hands on. Such smokers, having always waited impatiently for some other dope fiend to blow free smoke in their face, do not comprehend that cigarette smoke literally makes me sick, and get angry when I do not enjoy their exhalations. I therefore remove myself up wind. The males get it, the females do not.

On this particular morning there was a formerly attractive female begging to share cigarettes with strange men and women, and trying to sell bus tickets that she had gotten with some older dope fiend's senior discount card. She had a nice figure at about forty, though her skin screamed sixty, her posture twisted to seventy, and her voice was a halting crone-like ninety. She spotted me, and placing confidence in her still perky B-cups, croaked, "Hey hon? Hey Hon?!"

A man I would have glared at; warned off with a narrow gaze. With women I look away. She croaked her soot-clogged siren's call again and then limped over to me in a once perfect stripper-quality body, now apparently bent with agonizing constipation. She came up to me and I sneered and turned away as the ashcan scent wafted off of her toxic hair.

"Hey hon, I have a bus ticket. You need a bus ticket? Two dollars for a bus ticket. You are goin' to pay three-fifty. Save a dollar-fifty and help me out, please?"

I snarled, "I'm good", and looked away, never even seeing her face, refusing to acknowledge her humanity. If she were a male I would already be edging him toward the busy street for a push. But she was once female, maybe even a person, so I just erased her vile smell, her gnarled image from my mind as I open my Solomon Kane book and read about 'black fiends rising up from hell!'

She finally gets it, "Yer lyin'. You don' have a ticket. Yer mean."

Off she teetered toward the bus. She waited to watch me pay my $3.50, out of my last five for the week. I even let her see how thin my wallet was, that I would rather forgo lunch tomorrow, than to profit her a dime, parasite that she was. I soon found myself surrounded by working thirty-something and twenty-something blacks headed to low-paying jobs, seated alongside stoner forty-something whites headed to the government drug dispensaries, where your tax money is used to finance the suicides of my irritating co-commuters, and enrich the drug-dealers that serve them.

Late for Work [10:23 PM 8/12/13]

I woke an hour late for work as the power had cut out and disabled my clock. I had missed the last bus across town to Whitetrashistan. I got dressed and considered the recent drive-up attacks in my neighborhood as I stood over my footlocker. All of these attacks have been occurring in this time slot with the epicenter being the very bus stop I would be walking to. I pocketed a small pocketknife with a flip-posted two-inch blade.

As I walked west on the secondary road I live on, just past the spot where one of my neighbors was recently run down by a group of men, I spotted a young mohawked white-boy [18-19] on a BMX bike, checking his smart phone, and waiting beneath the 'Lawbreaker beware!' neighborhood watch sign.

Lawbreaker Beware [10:35 PM]

Walking towards him from the west, across the main drag, was a tall black youth without a shirt [unarmed, a cash or drug currier who would have muscle nearby]. As I emerged from the secondary street and crossed, I saw the white-boy dart from the alley that intersected the main and secondary streets on his BMX, peddling north into Whitebreadistan faster than anyone could run. It occurred to me that this boy was a mule—and a good one.

As I turned to check the ATM zone down the street for any raiders or drive-up bankers I noticed a large black man in his late twenties, dressed in cargo pants and double white T-shirts turning into the secondary street from the south. Soon the shirtless mover crossed the street to the western enclave. Seconds later the hitter emerged and headed south where he had come from, where the Pakistani farm store serves as a drug depot.

On the Bench [10:37-55 PM]

I take a seat at the bus stop on the west side of the main drag as another cargo pants wearing double T-shirt uniformed thug struts toward me, slows as he measures me—my hand under the flannel shirt that is draped on my lap—and continues on by with a nod, down south toward the pizzeria, bar, ATM, and farm store; the only businesses now open.

A cop drives by, and slows to look at me, continuing south.

A wiry black man in his twenties sees me from the east side of the street and crosses the street obliquely in front of me as he heads south. He asks me for a cigarette, and I say, "I don't smoke," and he continues on down the west side of the street.

The cop drives back north, slowing to observe me, and continues out of sight over the hill.

The bus comes, and I get up to board. It is ending at North Avenue and Asquith, one of the deadliest areas in town, right next to the Eastern District Courthouse. I need to get all the way downtown. I understand that the cop will be back and he, having never taken a bus—pussy mamma's boy whitebread bitch that he is—will not believe that I am still legitimately waiting for the bus. I take my pocket knife and drop it into the bottom of my man-purse.

Just then, coming up the street, is the thug returning, with no carry out items. He is either returning from the ATM, or a drug buy, or is going to give me trouble. I have no weapon. I focus on his neck, just staring at it, visualizing my leap for his throat with my teeth, the only weapon left to me thanks to my fear of the cop. He pats his side nervously with his right hand and eases on by as we glare at each other. He passes and then picks up his stride.

I then look to the south again and see a giant: a six-and-a-half-foot tall, muscular black man with a go-tee. He is in his mid-twenties and uniformed like the rest, his hand in his right side pocket, eyeing me intensely but not confrontationally. 'Shit', I think, 'I can't even get to his throat unless I knock him down and that's not happening. I'll shove my hand down his pants and tear his junk off.'

He has now slowed and is nervously moving something in his pocket. I'm thinking knife or .25 auto. He then glances ahead past me and nods respectfully to me and walks on by. I follow him up the sidewalk with my eyes and see him meet and greet a stoner white-boy in his forties. He takes his hand out of his pocket and uses that hand to shake hands with the wiry white-boy in his ball cap. They part, him continuing north as the white-boy passes me and nods as he pockets something.

I think these three actors comprise another drug deal, one for a personal quantity; again, two black customer-service providers and one white customer, just like Taco Bell.

The cop is now cruising south again. When he sees me still sitting at the bus he does a U-turn back north, and begins another U-turn on the west side. I just know he is going to be harassing me and am hoping that my cousin Cheri will be on duty at Central Booking so I don't get thrown in with a bunch of gangbangers to be beaten and raped. Just then the bus that I need comes over the hill and I board in a hurry as the cop U-turns up behind it.

'Fuck you White Pig!" I thought, as I thanked the elderly black driver, nodded to the elderly Church Lady, and went back to sit three seats forward of the young stoner white-boy, in his late twenties, who sat nervously on the edge of his seat, not relishing the trip into the deep ghetto below.

It occurs to me as I sit that the driver and I are two rare surviving versions of 1970s black men. It is nights like this that I realize that I am far, far 'blacker' as the term was used in my youth, than any of the modern hood-rats that now make that cultural claim. I am blacker even than this black bus driver who has basically become like a 1970s white man; a subspecies that is culturally all but extinct. No wonder BASH [Baltimore Area Skin Heads] employed that stoner white trash gang, the Wasted Youth, to assassinate me in the late 1980s.

The Church Bus [10:55-11:20 PM]

The young man moves up to sit across from me obliquely, him facing forward, me towards the back door, and asks, "How long for this bus to get downtown sir?"

"It's empty. We're on The Block in twenty. But those buses are headed out of town and will be packed."

"You catching the twenty-three home?"

"Yeah, but headed in—overslept."

We then continued with a bus route navigation discussion, comparing our longest walks, etc. Before the buses reached the condemned housing area being bought up by Johns Hopkins Hospital a ghetto lesbian gang-banger got on, uniformed like the thugs out the road: cargo shorts, double white T-shirts, scowl, shoulders threateningly sloped...

The Church Lady was now deep in a conversation with the driver from the 'rap seat'. I did not get his statements, only hers, "I feel so good after service—feel the Spirit of The Lord Jesus moving in me. It makes me wonder though about the world, when I meet people who fail to see the Spirit of The Lord in me. Does that mean I don't have enough faith, have not taken enough of The Lord in me? Sorry about running on but I'm high—high on church! What is up with this wiped out neighborhood? What happened here?"

The driver speaks, "Drugs, overrun with drugs!"

The lady then gets more animated. "You know what my pastor said the cure is, drug-testing for food stamps!"

The man across from me and the lesbo gangbanger up front both groaned out-loud. The Church Lady then turned her accusatory finger on the gang girl. "You know it's true girl—yer mamma on that drug stuff, her man on that drug stuff—en look at you!"

The gang girl turned all the way around and leaned away facing me across the back of her seat with anger in her face and tears in her eyes, as the Church Lady went on about drugs and parents.

I have a pretty good sense of what food stamps meant to this young thug girl when she was a child. If she was provided for by her mother in the same way as 7 out of 10 black children in Baltimore, this is how it went for her, and well explains the pain that soon sent her off the bus in tears, I believe before her destination...

As a supermarket manager I can attest to the following sequence of subsidy: the food stamp money hits town between the 6th and the 16th. Mamma then comes shopping with her children and her 'man'. The man generally has plenty of cash but spends it on liquor, dope and prostitutes, who spend it on dope. Mamma spends her money, first and foremost, on steamed shrimp, snow crab leg clusters, steaks, and decorated cakes; the former for her and her man, and the latter for her and her lady friends' get together. What is left of her money is used to purchase soft drinks, Kool-aid, sugar, prepackaged snack cakes, salty snack foods, hotdogs, frozen french-fries, and dried instant noodles. This child was most likely nutrient-starved her entire childhood, despite eating massive calories.

As the ghetto girl bailed off the bus the young man spoke up, "I'm on food stamps and methadone. I'm an Iraqi War veteran—three years protecting you in the Marine Corp—I have shrapnel in my legs from an IED!"

Church Lady: "Baby, you don't need that methadone, you need Jesus."

Marine: "You don't know what you're talking about!"

Church Lady: "Oh, you jus' hear what you wanna hear!"

Marine: "I was protecting you—thank you very much."

Church Lady: "You weren't protecting me, you was killin' blacks."

Marine: "Are you fuckin' retarded bitch!"

It is now our stop and we are getting off at The Block. As we do the Church Lady yells, "Come here and say that en I will slap the shit outa a yer ass white-boy!"

We are now laughing on the sidewalk heading to the transfer point, and he is fired up and rambling, "White-boy, white-boy! Hear that?"

"It didn't take long to scrape the church off of her."

"It doesn't take much to bring out the animal in people. These blacks crack me up. [We are now crossing to the bum-strewn south side of The Block looking for our bus.] They're the first ones to go Moslem and they think that's being 'black', that Moslems are black. I killed Moslems as white as you over there. Fuckin' bitch isn't speaking Arabic is she? How would she feel if I shattered her face! I'm headed to Royal Farms for some cigarettes. I'll meet you at the stop."

The strippers, barkers, gangsters and cops are back to my left. Ahead is the transfer point and the army of sprawled homeless men living on the sidewalk.

The Block [11:20-11:45 PM]

I pass more heavily laden bums stretched out on the sidewalk. Black children and youths are walking all over the place in groups, peacefully having a good time. At the transfer point is a shapely lady in black spandex shorts and a low cut T-shirt, dancing to her head set. She lives in a world without fear, as there is only one thing that men want from her, and she is obviously willing to give that away.

A grungy white trash alcoholic about my age approaches me, fouling my view of the rotating hips. "Got a cigarette you can spare boss?"

"I don't smoke man."

"Good for you brother."

He then steps back to get a better view of our dancer, nods approvingly, and then leans on the fencing to relax until the bus rolls up. We are all—except the bike boy—obviously Eastside people waiting on the #23.

There is also a young go-tee boy with a bike, who is on call to provide some kind of service for someone, as he keeps checking his smart phone, as we three take turns checking her out. I have fallen back into the shadows so no one can get behind me, and so that the other young lady—a retail employee—will not feel uncomfortable about me being so close. Bike boy and I are both keeping our distance from the women.

A group of youths come by and proposition the dancer and she moves more seductively, but looks away with her chin up, indicating that they are inadequate. Her dance, however, did not fail to educate. As a dedicated man of science I forced myself, despite the insult to my puritanical ethos, to count her wiggles. Keep in mind that she was built more for roller derby than the dance floor, with a striking structural similarity to tennis star Serena Williams. I discovered, through diligent scientific analysis, that every 4.5 rotations of her ample hips required the manipulation of her constricting shorts, less they eventually bunch up into an unseemly G-string. The lady did, after all, have her dignity to maintain.

The Insanity Bus [11:45 PM-12:30 AM]

The #23 is packed with 49 people, 4 more than it seats. I get the post stand by the back door and observe. The gangbangers crowding the back deck of the bus are discussing, 'Lowdown chumpass niggas', 'hot hos', 'babyback bitchez' 'crushin dat piss-test' 'smokin' blunts' 'drinkan liquor' 'beatin chargez' and other such philosophic topics of the day.

In another block, 7 board, including the Marine, who stays up front. A family of six, including an infant, toddler, and two young children are to the right. To the left is a mamma and her two older children, one of whom befriends the Marine.

We roll for a half mile, stop and let 1 off and take on 6, including a hot little girl in almost nothing and her huge cock-blocker wearing a tent like pink dress, who is holding out her middle finger to a group of teenage boys on the sidewalk. The hottie sits on her cock-blocker's lap and the drones up behind me begin a chorus, of 'Yo babbay—I got yo lap right hea', and other such chivalrous talk. One of the leaders of this clique is a small mouthy dread-locked scumudgeon who tries to hit on her.

More people load. This is tough in the ghetto where bumping a shoe can get you shot. So there is many a needless apology. Saturation-level survival courtesy is practiced by all but myself, as I don't buy into apologizing for incidental human contact in order to avoid being shot.

We are now headed up the Eastside and 'Minze', the dread-locked thirty-something featherweight stooge who wants to mate with this 15-year-old girl, is becoming the center of attention. He is utterly drunk out of his mind and desperately hanging onto his last full-sized cigarette, which alternately finds purchase behind his greasy locks, in his mouth, and between his dirty fingers. He drops the cigarette no fewer than three times while standing next to me. Each time he is unable to reach it and pleads pathetically with good cancer-promoting Samaritans, "Dat be minze yo—please yo, fish dat shit up!"

Eventually we swing into Highlandtown and he rings the bell, breaking his savory cig in half. The driver—unable to hear in the 70-person din—misses the stop and he begins to yell, "Yo, yo. Wo, yo yo—Minze, babbay Minze!"

He now wants to get off between stops and she says, "Baby, I will hook you up in a moment."

"Oh, I'm not havin' dat disrespect yo!"

Our heroic mating drone now decides to challenge the ruling matriarchy and worms his way up through the standing passengers, holding up our progress as he heads to the captain's chair to protest. Just as he turns toward her rather than exiting I and others groan. His revolution is short-lived, as her hand, the girth of his scrawny head, waves in his face and she directs him, "I said have a safe trip baby—don't make me say it again."

He did his best Snoop Dog imitation as he strutted out into the world and we pulled off toward Greek Town and the hospital. More and more people board and offload, and I begin to hear the bus driver giving specific security instructions for those who offload. The Harm City Police Department has, instead of alarming the public through the media, been notifying the pedestrians that have borne the brunt of our recent wave of violent crime, through bus operators. She reminds everyone: "Look out for suspicious people; do not give out change or cigarettes, conceal your smart phone, do not speak on your cell phone, and do not listen to you head set while walking. Be careful and have a safe night."

This is all good Harm City advice.

As people offload I move to a central seat and catch a snippet of the nine-year-old boy's conversation with the Marine. He turns and tells his mamma, "He was a Marine Mamma, served in Iraq—in the war!"

The lady waved to him, "Thank you sir, thank you!"

The Marine beamed and shook hands with the boy before getting off at the famous Broadway Diner at Kane Street.

At East Point Mall a squishy egg-shaped white male in his early twenties boards with a bag. He is doing the 'dope-fiend lean', an obvious opiate user. He sits down across from me, behind the family of six. He begins to nod, then produces one of those mechanical tobacco oil cigarettes and takes a drag. I hate that these things are legal because something in the oil, some chemical in the tobacco extract, makes me nauseous, just like the actual burned pollutant. I brace for the reek as the smoke streams up on either side of his head and the family members in front of him cover their mouths and the baby's mouth with shirts.

But it is not that tobacco oil. It is something vaguely sweet I remember smelling three decades ago when I was drinking with a biker who was helping four strippers fire heroin. One of the girls was afraid of the needle and he had her smoke the heroin from a hash pipe. This smelled like that, and Humpty Junky nodded immediately off into oblivion.

Just Past Midnight in the Garden of Sloth [12:30-12:51 AM

I offload with two youths, a tough looking bald dude, and Serena, who struts her substantial stuff westward as the bald dude and I walk northeast and the youths head east, with warnings to safeguard our person and hide our valuables still ringing in our ears.

I lose track of the bald dude so fish out my knife and pocket it, worried that I'm too old to handle him with my hands. He has disappeared and the park soon looms on my left. I catch movement to my left and duck noise to my right. To my left, across the street, is Clown Face and her three drones, who follow her about with their gothic makeup, 'I'm not completely gay yet yellow backpacks' and skateboards. Clown Face is in her teens, has a sad clown tattooed on her face, and has well over fifty facial piercings. She looks revolting and is rather shapeless, but attracts a steady stream of worshippers. One can only imagine what vile things she does to achieve this cult like status. Her lips and eyebrows are so pierced they look like zippers.

I pass a handful of punks smoking reefer outside the 7-ll. The cops usually hit this place for free food and drink at midnight, and it is well past that; a cop-free drug den once again.

I pass through the mini-park near the riverbank where the local homeless retarded lady camps out. I am fast closing in on the two I suspect provided the drugs now being enjoyed by Clown Face and her southbound company, and the suburban stoners at the 7-11. This pair is ambling slowly, as the big muscular black one is so wide he cannot progress forward easily. His companion is a tiny bald white-boy with a disgustingly moist smoker's cough. I call these fellows Muscle & Mucus.

I am two hours late for work. If I waltz at their pace I will lose another quarter hour of wages. They are crossing the bridge and I will not step off into the road so overtake them. They narrow up and make way for me and I pass on the bridge, making my way to work at Mister John's Market.

I punch in just in time to see two late teenage junkies making love in the meat aisle. The female is so stoned out of her mind that she is drooling on the floor, long strings of saliva yo-yoing from her mouth as the tattooed freak who is kissing her is holding his head between her hands and saying, "I love you baby; love…Remember that baby, love!"

She lets out this barely audible canine-like whimper and gurgles on her pooling saliva as they hug and she blows a spit bubble on his shoulder, the T-bone steaks [which sell good at food stamp time] they were selecting forgotten behind them, dropped in the intake slot where they tumbled when this postmodern Romeo and Juliette fell into their touching embrace.

There you go: a Monday night in Harm City. Tours are twenty dollars an hour, and may be booked by leaving a request below using the comment feature, and making a deposit next to that picture of my faithful assistant Charles at the top right of this blog page.

All aboard!

Snapshots of a Stoned World

Charm City

The Brighter Side of Baltimore

© 2012 James LaFond

I live and work in Baltimore and environs, and hence generally see a much darker side of Baltimore than the typical tourist. Indeed most violent crime takes place not on special event dates [like the flash mob attacks that were the focus of *Stoning Baboons*], but under normal circumstances. Predators prefer predictable prey and a constant habitat. Of course a large number of soft unprotected targets, such as the Saint Valentine's Eve tourists who were pack attacked by hundreds of Baltimorean thugs will be selected when available.

Narco Night Train

From Thursday June 14th thru this evening, Saturday the 16th, I escorted two out-of-town friends around Baltimore City. I have often poked fun at the term Charm City that was coined when Baltimore was developed as a tourist attraction in the early 1980s, even adopting the sarcastic moniker ascribed to it by its violent youth. So, I descended into this touristy abyss with some curiosity. It was an odd experience for me. Normally I see the city between nightfall and sunrise on work days when little security is in evidence. On this weekend the Navy's Blue Angels and an international flotilla of 'tall ships' brought in huge crowds of polite sober families, ushered by many hundreds of security guards and watched over by at least four law enforcement agencies. Even tactical units and Homeland Security was on station.

The contrast was stunning. I did not see a panhandler and the bums laid low. Even the occasional drug dealers were well behaved as they paraded their prized fighting dogs and scantily clad consorts. Criminals, after all, deserve a holiday too. The government presence came close to a national disaster cleanup effort and stifled any violence. With the city swelled to twice its normal population it ran smoother than ever in the commercial district that is normally a prime hunting ground, where I have had homeless men follow me zombie-like on winter nights moaning for the coat off of my back.

This is clear evidence that human predators are creatures of habit who adapt poorly to sudden changes in hunting conditions and policing. A large part of this disruption of violence was the sudden large influx of cohesive mixed-age and mixed-gender groups. There were very few preoccupied individuals rushing to and fro.

Local and federal law-enforcement did a good job enabling us to stand beneath the thundering jet fighters and thank Allah that we weren't driving a Toyota pickup packed with suspected terrorists across a dusty Afghan road. Ultimately, though, I would have to say the key was those tens of thousands of men and women who were holding doors, and hands, and making sure that the old, young and crippled were all taken care of first. The average person was vigilant and kind. Nothing has more of an impact on violent crime.

When some unusual event causes people to forget to buy into the politics of alienation that dominates their modern work-a-day world they begin to look out for one another and the criminals take a step back and bide their time. The next time we have a blizzard or the ships come into your town, enjoy it; experience what life could be if we were normally politely vigilant. To me this past weekend was a dream-time during which I could fantasize that everything my parents taught me about people being naturally good was true, like sniffing that one special flower that blooms infrequently.

Fat City

Notes on Postmodern Livestock Management

© 2012 James LaFond

"If I see one more three-hundred-pound woman in hot pants I'm going to barf! One woman's confidence is another woman's disgust." - supermarket clerk

Bath-salt Barbarians

I have often used the food metaphor to identify the 'victims' or targets of aggression. Recently folks who keep up on the news, which I do not, have congratulated me on my prophetic assertion that modern human society is essentially cannibalistic. Apparently, so I am told, various freaks up and down the East Coast are snorting something called bath-salts and then eating each other. I will never go shopping for my sister at Bed Bath & Beyond without feeling like Stephan King again.

It has occurred to me—recently that is, when I was beseeched by the supermarket clerk quoted above, that we are really just livestock. She wanted to know if she was wrong, even apologizing for her lack of tolerance of unashamedly dressed morbidly obese people. I, crank social Darwinist that I am, blurted—well, coming from me it sounded like sage commentary—that these fat people are not to be blamed. They are just livestock being bred and fattened by the State and corporations in collusion. Modern society, I said, is nothing but 'people farming'. Our natural omnivorous primate impulse to consume coupled with our curiosity and status consciousness is the driver for our economy, which is largely built on feeding, clothing, hauling and entertaining us. To me, powered wheel-chairs is the metaphor for humanity's future—our destination.

In the meantime, until you too have become a prisoner beneath your own subsidized blubber, here are some survival tips on managing your fellow humans, who have, like Odysseus's crew, been reduced to grubbing livestock...

The Gelatinous Shield

They make mass transit tough, taking up two and three seats at a time. But, what a human shield! Many a Middle Eastern terrorist would like to have one of these for a firing post. Squeeze in next to the food-stamp beneficiary and use them as a crash pad when the bus wrecks, or at the bus stop use them to shield you against wind, rain, menthol cigarette smoke, and 9MM slugs.

The One Man Crowd

I have worked crowd control where 30% of the controlees were morbidly obese and 10% were two to three chairs wide. You cannot push them with your hands. They are however, by nature weak-willed and sensitive. If you can get them upset enough at you to move away, all you have to do is stand opposite from the direction you want the rest of the people to move, and your one-man-crowd will move them for you. The skinny ones that eddy around their mass are easy to pick off and shove into their ponderous wake.

Suggestion Box Sally

Once I worked at a market that had a pretty blonde security guard who boasted [well, she did not actually boast about it] an enormous posterior. Her butt was three feet wide. She used to lay her torso face down on the belt of the last register with her butt facing the front door while she read magazines and ate ice cream cones. We had a suggestion box by the front door. One customer wrote, "Please, remove the giant ass from register 15. I am getting sick of seeing it every time I come through the front door."

The night captain dutifully moved the 'giant ass' to a folding chair in the drug aisle and posted the owner of said posterior there to yell when she saw a shoplifter. When Sally told him that she didn't yell [I don't either] he said, "Then you can moo or squeal, I don't give a shit. Just make noise."

Later that week we grabbed a small skinny man trying to leave with ill-gotten goods.

The night captain asked Sally, as she rolled up front on the handicapped cart, to throw him her handcuffs. She said, "I forgot them."

He said, "Well then sit your fat ass right here! Sit on this piece-of-shit while I call the cops!"

As the night captain kept the 120 lb shoplifter pinned down by pressing his forehead to the floor Sally took a seat on the shoplifter's lower back. The man howled in protest, "Oh Gawd yo! Dis big bitch be breakin' my back yo. I's gonna be crippled yo! I's, suin' dis joint—Good Gawd yo! I'm dyin' unda dis fat bitch!"

I have rarely laughed that hard. Sally was not feeling merciful, and actually ground her butt onto the man's back who had made the mistake of insulting her while she had him in a double reverse cowgirl mount.

I work in an industry that has thrived by selling high-fat, high-carb, high-sodium foods and beverages to low-income, low-IQ people who buy this stuff with my tax dollars. I see nothing wrong with using the resulting body-mass to gain a survival advantage.

James LaFond, July 4th 2012

Crime and Payment

A Brief Memoir of a Teenage Drug Dealer

© 2012 James LaFond

Caley is a stocky, tattooed, long-haired young man who, just last month, finally earned the right to drink alcohol by surviving the requisite 21 years of enforced sobriety mandated by our benevolent oligarchs. That is not to say that he is ignorant of the ways of intoxication. As unlikely as it seems, of all of the many drug dealers I have interviewed, Caley is not only the youngest but the smartest— and he's already retired. Talk about an exit strategy. If only he had been selling weed to the Iraqi's George W. Bush might not have looked like such a fool.

Like most highly intelligent people Caley was easy to collar for an interview. You see, smart people tend to be lonely for that someone they can explain themselves to and Caley is no different; living the smart man's curse, exiled to his desert Island of Introspection amid the vast Ocean of Stupidity that he was born into and remains to lap its lonely shore...

Mom

My mother named me Caledonia Aloysious; set me up for failure from the start by consigning me to a life of beatings. I guess Caley is an improvement. Mom had that nickname planned from the beginning.

This should really be about her. She had the hard way to go—spent thirteen years getting raped and beaten until she moved out on the streets with us kids. She worked so didn't qualify for any food stamps or welfare or any of that shit. We had nowhere to live, nowhere! I was about ten. I really can't get into it or I'll start crying. [Caley was really uncomfortable about discussing this portion of his childhood. I did note early on in our series of 7 interviews that he had a hard time placing his age when recalling his childhood experiences, and that he tended to divide everything into 'before ten' or 'after ten'.]

After I started making money and sent her to a NASCAR event some guy hits on her and she beats his ass. She really turned things around. I always did good in school because my mother would have killed me if I flunked or dropped out. Actually school was really easy.

Pop

I don't remember much before ten [years of age]. I guess I blocked a lot out. The first abuse thing I can remember—hell, maybe it is the first thing I can remember—must of happened when I was two or three. We were at my uncle's house on my mom's side. Dad en Mom got in an argument and my dad picked me up and took me to leave. Pop—my grandfather on my Mom's side—came outside and grabbed my dad by the throat with one hand and pressed him up against the truck. Pop was big, real thick like a bear, definitely over three-hundred. Dad was maybe two-twenty. I remember him holding my dad off the ground with one hand while he took me with the other hand and handed me to Mom. I was maybe three, and that's pretty much how my childhood went.

Poppy Tom

My dad's dad was in bad shape. He was dyin' from heart trouble and cancer, even had a sensor in his bedroom. His great-grandmother was a hundred percent Indian: Cherokee and something else. He was teaching my brother and me what his grandmother had taught him, wanted to pass it on. He used to hunt and made the leather himself out of the hides. He made my brother and me a matching set of leather wallets, with our Indian names embossed in them. He also liked to make ice cream out of snow. I remember a big snowfall just before he died. We used to bring the snow into his bedroom and he would make the ice cream.

One day I went into his bedroom to wake him up. I said, 'Poppy Tom wake up.'

I got my mom and they came and said he wasn't breathing. I was little. It was definitely before I was ten. The stuff he made for my brother and I; my father, he kept it and I don't associate with him [*clenches jaw*].

Bro

My brother was a couple years older than me. We did a lot together. By the time I was a teenager he had the kind of reputation that meant people didn't mess with me. We did a lot of stuff together when we were little and I think had a pretty normal life in school and outside. It was at home that things were messed up.

One time before we were ten we were digging a hole in the yard and spreading sand, for putting in a pool. There was this neighborhood kid helping us. I don't remember his name. I don't remember much about the day really. The kid asked me a question. I don't remember what the question was but I answered 'no'. The kid was using a heavy ground rake and just clocked me with it. All I remember was falling back with my eyes closing and seeing my brother punching him. The next thing I knew I was waking up in the hospital and eating vanilla wafers. It was right under the hairline on the left [*shows two inch scar under hairline above right eye*] and lifted a piece of bone out. I had a lot of stitches.

A couple of years later we were at my grandma's house playing outside. This kid came out of nowhere, jumped from behind this tree, and slammed this board with a rusty nail sticking out of it into my head. We had asked him where his brother was. We were just playing, and I think they were hitting everybody like that and I don't think the kid new about the nail—like he intentional stuck it in my head. It was on the top of the head and [came down] from the side. My brother beat the shit out of him—a pretty bad beating.

I guess I've got a pretty hard head. There was one time my cousin slammed my head in a car door by accident—tore off the top half of my right ear. It was just an accident. He was like a brother two; my mom raised him too. So I came up taking a lot of ass-kickings.

Dad

Dad and Mom's room was downstairs. Our rooms were upstairs. He used to think it was funny to call us downstairs and then throw full cans and bottles of soda at us, even two-liters. There was a lot of verbal abuse. He would beat us every day. I thought it was normal to be honest. It wasn't that he had an aggressive personality. He had a lot of friends; firemen and cop buddies. But behind closed doors it was different. He had a 'Jekyl and Hide' personality.

Really, the most disturbing thing he ever did to me was tell me that my mother didn't love me because she wanted a girl and that she used to try and kill me when I was a baby because I wasn't a girl. He used to take our money and give it to our youngest sister. There were four of us, my brother and me and our two younger sisters.

We did try to fight back. He had a stomach problem and couldn't digest certain kinds of food. He also had bad knees. He didn't have a job and if he did it didn't last for long. Mom worked between two and four jobs supporting us four kids. Now every day he would belt us; fist, open hand, belt, whatever he could get his hands on. Sometimes when he was sleeping we would smack his stomach or kick his knees. We'd get beat the worse for it but it was worth it.

On one occasion he threw one of those folding wooden tray-tables at us and it almost hit my little sister. She was real young when he threw the table. That was the day we left; no place to go, just out on the street, away from him.

Weed

I did not start getting high until long after I started selling. As a drug it's appealing because it is less toxic than cigarettes and far less harmful than alcohol to those around you. To die from smoking pot you'd have to lock yourself in an unventilated room. Even then you would die from the same thing that kills old ladies in house fires—the smoke and carbon monoxide.

When I was fifteen a friend of mine—a real good friend, closer even then my brother and we're close—was selling. I was always good at talking to people so I started setting up deals for him—like a broker. I'm not using, buying, selling so I'm a clean fix. When he started getting weight [quantities sufficient for distribution] I started buying from him.

At first there might be a one-ounce day or maybe it took me three days to unload an ounce. People don't get into selling pot because of the bulk—of course—and because they think there is no money in it. That's wrong, and just shows you how stupid most people are. Coke is all cutup and mashed down as far as it can go when it comes into town, nothing left to cut. Pills are really the only thing that is as popular as weed and they all have fixed prices. Everybody knows what you paid for it and you are just selling the same perk or oxy as the next guy.

But with pot, it is an organic product grown around the world with a lot of variance in quality. You've got all kinds of crazy shit coming into the country and also what is being grown.

If you have a good connect and have quality product you just mark it up accordingly.

Most people screw up on their inventory control. Yeah, I kept a stash, everybody keeps a stash. Hiding one thing is not so hard. But breaking it up and moving it out will get you burned. People don't sell bags of pot like back in your old-ass day...

...Back to the weight; a scale gets you five years! That's a distribution charge right there. Now the 'old-head' way of measuring was done with the finger [makes a hook out of index finger] but I have small hands. I only moved an eigth of an ounce at a time. That way if you get busted it doesn't carry a distribution charge.

Now nobody buys weight they buy blunts. A blunt is a cheap cigar. You take a knife and split it down the side. You rip out the leaf—that shit is poison and you throw it away. You push the weed in. Leave a little bit of tobacco at the bottom and some on the end and roll it back up. An eighth rolls four blunts.

I would buy a couple ounces at a time and kept a stash but only broke out an eighth to go sell. That is very important—not to move weight. It is a discipline. An eighth costs forty [$40] for 'mids' [standard grade]; basically ten dollars per blunt. I would sell an eighth of 'mids' for fifty to eighty, depending on who it was. My man was getting crazy good shit though. That is where the money comes in, when you have the quality product: Afghan Kush, African Kush, Great Granddad Perp—all kinds of crazy shit. You smoke some of it with them to demonstrate the quality.

So, with an eighth of exotic weed I'm spending sixty to one-thirty-five and selling it for one-forty-five to two-forty. I tried not to deal in 'mids' too much. I'd text him [the supplier] 'Is everything good?' If he said 'yeah, come by the house' then I knew he had what I needed. We'd chill, play some games, have a drink. I'd always smoke his weed, not mine. When I was buying I always smoked before the purchase, when it was his shit. When I was selling I always smoked after the purchase, when it was their shit.

Now somebody would text me—I never talked on the phone—and ask 'are you good?' We would then meet at their house if it was a friend, at a park, or at the McDonald's in the bathroom. It would depend on who they were and where I was at. If someone called or asked for weight I knew something was up [wrong].

My best three-days of sales was two-thousand net. A week usually brought me twelve-hundred to two-thousand in profit. I had a job the whole time. It was easy money. I would spend only three hours a week sometimes and make four times what I made at my full-time job. [He was working and still attending high school.] If you do it for a while you gain some knowledge and don't let yourself get caught up in stupid shit. I did not deal with people I didn't know. You don't walk up to someone in the street like these coons do now and say, 'Grass is out.' That's how you get caught or beat-up and robbed.

I had two things going for me: cops and criminals. I had some cop friends who would call me up and let me know when and where busts were going down, even if it was just a house party that was being broken up, so that I wouldn't get caught up in it. I learned that from my father. He had cop friends that made sure my mother's brutality and abuse charges never made it anywhere. It's like that. I also had my cousin and my brother who were just crazy fighters who people didn't want to mess with, and a couple of friends who had done time for murder and were out. So people that knew me didn't really consider robbing me. The one guy worked for the Bloods, and used to make his victims tie themselves up with their own shoelaces. [Sounds like tying together of shoes to hobble a hostage, but it was third-person so I didn't inquire.]

To this day I can't even walk to the Seven-Eleven without getting harassed by cops. I have never been arrested or charged but I have been stopped a lot. One day my friends and I had been partying so we decided to walk up to the McDonalds and get something to eat. At the top of the street three or four cop cars come flying up and screech on the breaks. They're piling out. One has a night stick and one has a tazer. They tell my friends to leave. They had me walk towards them with my hands up. The one cop then bent my arm behind my back. Then he grabbed me by the hair and the belt loop and heaved my fat ass up off the ground and slammed me on the hood. I said, 'What's this about?'

The cop said, 'Don't worry, it's not about drugs. You just fit the description of a rapist seen running out of the woods after a girl was raped.'

I was like, 'Oh shit, that wasn't me!'

Another cop pulled up and asked, 'Is that the guy?'

The cop in the car looked at a picture, and said, 'You got the wrong guy.'

That's when I started having fun with them. I was holding my neck, talking about lawyers, and my friends were giving them shit about they saw the brutality. The cops got nervous and then just apologized and let me go.

I was eighteen and the risks started getting to be too much. When you get into this you have to abide by the TYC rule: 'Take Your Charge'. If you get pinched you take it like a man and do your time. You don't roll over on somebody else because you were a dumbass.

Well, there was this guy who I basically put out of business when I started selling. He got busted with three ounces and a scale—that's jail time. I began to notice that people he did business with were getting busted. I also noticed he didn't have any pending court dates. A cop buddy of mine called me up and said, 'They are coming for you.'

I had a friend take my stash. Then this guy, the dumbass with the scale, calls me up and says, 'Hey, you want to hang out?'

I told him I'd stop by. I got stopped on the way over. Now, these were [Baltimore] County Cops, and they don't like being wrong, so I knew they'd be on me. They still are three years after I stopped dealing. Now the guy, the dumbass with the scale, he ended up getting beat up real bad. I don't know what happened but he did have to eat with a straw for almost a year. He didn't mind his TYC.

A Special Fear: A Related Perspective on Narcotics & Cops

I once interviewed a heroin dealer in the city. He was an interesting character who got started in crime at age ten, when he was employed by the owners of a shoe store to run numbers deposits and payments around his neighborhood in a shoebox. He got involved in martial arts and developed a creed. When he was approached by the Chapter President of the Pagans Motorcycle Club to train his people, he declined, thinking it would be a stain on his teacher's art. He eventually got involved in his brother's heroin business and took it over after his death.

When I asked him about the scariest aspect of his business he told me that it was the cops; not the cops that arrest you, but the ones that come over to your supplier's house three at a time to snort coke, and the guy that ran him out of business; a police lieutenant who retired, bought a bar, and then took over the local heroin market. He told me, "Between the hospitals peddling their dope—from the so-called treatment centers—and keeping your customers addicted to their shit, you have the cops cutting in and taking over the business. I got out as soon as I found out the lieutenant put a price on my head. I got off the dope too—cold turkey. I was not going to get addicted to the hospital's shit."

Conclusion

This article is the product of seven interviews with Caley and one with Tim. If you are not interested in the subject I understand. For me it was something all-together new so I found it enlightening. I felt it was important to have an inside piece on some portion of the drug trade in *Harm City*. Because, it is in large measure the drug trade and the government's war on drugs that has made Baltimore the dangerous place that it is. Even though Caley was involved with low-level trafficking of arguably the most benign of illicit drugs, violence was always just a phone call away.

Also, if you are a reader of my violence books and articles I thought it would be useful to demonstrate the process. I conducted similar series of interviews with hundreds of people over the past 16 years, but the reader of the finished product just gets glimpses of their lives. Caley was not really that interested in speaking about his drug-trafficking. That was where my interest was. As the prying researcher I had to strike a compromise; a compromise that I think results in a broader, deeper picture being drawn from his words. He really didn't know me very well and seemed to regard me as something of a 'creepy old dude'. He was, however, needful of unlimbering some of his life experiences. You can see places where he drew back from the process and distanced himself. These hint at an unspoken subtext and can make for the focus of an eye-opening re-read.

Since I entered this process of recording violent urban oral histories from the perspective of wanting to understand the entire phenomena the approach quickly took on this comprehensive aspect. Hopefully this gives the reader a better understanding of the means by which the information in my non-fiction works has been acquired.

Narco Night Train

A Pack of Camels

Anecdote

© 2012 James LaFond

"I have these Baltimorean sensibilities that simply will not go away. Once you live in Harm City, Harm City lives in you."

-e-mail from an exiled Baltimorean hip-hopster

I was picking out my drink early this morning at a 7-11 just below the city line. Then in came a man who was obviously shaken. The clerk behind the counter said, "Are you okay man?"

The man, looking ashen and manic, exclaimed, "I haven't smoked a cigarette in four years, but I'm smokin' a whole pack of camels tonight!"

As I got in line behind him the clerk, veteran of numerous robberies, sensed a brush with violence, and took a calming approach, "What happened?"

Narco Night Train

"I was at the light, waiting to cross Moravia on Harford, when these three dudes come running out into the street shooting at someone. They're shooting and we—me and the cars behind—are backed up and can't get out! Jesus! They run on, blasting away, and I U-ey back up this way—flag down a cop. Know what the cop says? He says, 'get in and go back down with me'."

"Fuck that! I'm not goin' back down there! He gave me a number and told me to call in a complaint about the shooting."

Heads where shaken and transactions completed.

It rained an hour later, rained hard. I imagine, sitting here in the rain this morning, a few blocks away from the scene, that any blood spilled might have already drained into the Chesapeake Bay; the city's signature behavior becoming one with it's greatest natural resource.

James LaFond, Friday, October 19, 2012

Sloth in the City

Why Vice is Good for Self-defense

© 2012 James LaFond

Last night, 10/24/12, between 10:29 and 10:48 PM, I shared a city bus stop with two incompetent breeders. The female was the dominant partner. She was about 5'6" and 270 pounds, dressed to dance, and dance she did—in the gutter. Her consort was a dumpy less plump version of herself minus the huge breasts and mass of artificial hair. He attended her heap of luggage and pined for her attention with pine needles plucked from the overhanging tree behind them; brushing her twenty inch arms like a twelve-year-old with a crush on his best friend's older sister.

This unfortunately mated pair had, by the hopeful looks they cast my way, been at the stop for some time. She asked me if I came for the bus. I nodded, 'yes'. If they had been behaving decently I might have informed them that they would never be picked up. There were three reasons for this: they were at the head of the stop, just where the bus begins to bank, 20 yards from the boarding area; they were behind a big white working van and hence all but invisible; and, in case they were hoping to be rescued by a kindly bus operator, the bus driver that handles this route at this time likes his chocolate short and petite, not overstuffed.

The bus I did not want rumbled by, and did not stop for them due to the aforementioned reasons. They were upset, in a nice ignorant way, and acted in a bemused fashion. The female said to me, "Were you waiting for that bus?"

I nodded, 'no'.

I then began considering whether I should educate these apparent mass transit novices in the ways of the road. I wrestled with my conscience as the girl smiled plaintively at me. Then she began to dance again, and her consort threw their empty Mountain Dew bottle in the gutter beneath her prancing—booted—feet like she was some gypsy queen smashing liquor bottles under her heels. Thanks to their sloth I felt better about not helping them out.

Moments later we saw the next bus coming our way and they cheered. She even stepped out from behind the van and flagged down the bus. The bus grew nearer and then banked into the loading zone [indicated by a 20 yard concrete slab] to pick me up. Behind the bus on the sidewalk they struggled with their luggage and screamed about suing the MTA as he pulled off. I sat down to read the Koran next to this evangelical African Christian chick who is forever reading her Bible while everyone else listened to their earphone devices.

I have pointed the folks above out to you, not because I disliked them. They were likable in their own empty way, and meant me no ill will, indeed tried to befriend me. I pointed them out to you because they, in their sloth, are harmless to me, and, at the same time, easy pickings for whichever type of predator might have been out looking for someone to victimize. When you are on the menu it is nice to be placed next to something softer, tastier, with a higher caloric content, that is so much easier to chew...

An Insult to Animals

This morning I bypassed my first stop, even though I was tired, because I did not want to share any part of my early morning hours with 'Mister Suave', the name I have given to the young Latino man who I share the bus stop with in front of the Chinese eatery. Mister Suave dresses like a dandy, chain smokes, and spits constantly. He also insists on boarding first and inevitably causes the rest of us to wait as he extracts his bunched up cologne-soaked bills from beneath the band of his silk underwear. This morning I eschewed the suave life. After all, the air is cleaner on the way to the next stop.

Upon arrival at the first stop on the next line, a mile down the road, I was confronted by a huddled mass of humanity at the stop. This stop is a major transfer point and is therefore awash in litter. The landscape is literally a moonscape of soda bottles, cigarette wrappers and candy bar wrappers. I normally—and I'm not the only one—stand across the lot or even across the street until the bus comes to avoid the noxious ever-billowing cloud of mentholated cigarette smoke that engulfs this tiny ruined corner of the world.

This morning I stood particularly far away, as a 60-year-old white man, who I know to be a fast-food worker, managed to smoke his death-stick, pick his nose, spit, and blow his nose freeform into the air, all in perfect syncopation. This man is the B. B. King of bodily effusion. This is such a normal bus stop occupation, that even the pretty ladies in their suits and dresses, headed to work at hospitals and universities, did not even step aside as he flung his nasal excrement to and fro. In fact, three other patrons were spitting. Mind you, none of these folks were eating sunflower seeds major-league-baseball style or chewing tobacco. People in Baltimore just spit a lot because...they spit a lot. Standing in the gutter mere feet away a young man wolfed down a candy bar, sucking the chocolate from his fingers. Behind the ladies more men smoked and spit...

Why do I mention these slothful creatures in a column dedicated to urban survival and self-defense?

The reason is, I have found, through decades of experience, that practitioners of sloth are easily discouraged and defeated. The dedicated survivalist or self-defense practitioner looks at every gathering of humans as a lineup of potential adversaries; just as the predator views those same vapid souls as a menu of available prey. It seems antisocial—and I suppose is. However, the mental discipline it takes to look briefly at every person you encounter and size them up like a corner-man sizing up his fighter's opponents, imparts the ability to assess your options on the cuff on those rare occasions when those who share your habitat decide to threaten or attack you. It also takes you off the menu.

That last point is clutch. There were 15 people at this stop. Three of us stood off. There was me. There was also a really big man who did not want to blow his smoke in other people's faces—even though they were already being engulfed—and came to sit downwind from me. That man is someone who demonstrates courtesy at every level of his decision making, and a person I would aid. He is also not going to beg money from me or mug me.

Then there was the other guy, the short muscular guy who paced a lot, stayed behind the stop, and sized everyone up. He is dangerous. He might just be an antisocial survivor like me. Or he might be deciding who he is going to 'bank' when they cut through the parking garage on the other side of town where this bus is headed. He spared me a few glances, perhaps making the same assessment of me as I had of him. The point is, when you size-up those around you habitually it makes you aware, and, to those who size-up others for good or ill, it broadcasts your awareness; taking you off the prey menu. And that is just the ancillary affect of your awareness.

Oral Sloth

What about the slothful? Certainly there will arise from among their degenerate ranks, a violent person; a criminal. Perhaps he is just a panhandler that gets out of hand. Perhaps Mister Noxious Nose Nugget, having spewed all of his 60-year-old mucus at your lunch-spot kitchen, finally gets fired, gets drunk, and heads back this way, on your bus—next to you. Perhaps he breaks nasal on you?

Perhaps Mister Suave, on one fine morning, misjudges the wind, and spits on you. Perhaps you decide to let the pregnant woman board the bus ahead of Mister Suave, and he has a problem with that, and directs his Suavity at you?

This brings us back to the practical nature of sizing up every man and youth as a potential adversary. This is not limited to imagining a physical kinetic ending to your adversarial relationship. All such encounters are best kept sub-physical. Mister Noxious Nose Nugget could have a heart attack brought on simply by the strain of punching you.

Mister Suave wears five hundred dollars worth of clothes. You do not want, after pleading mutual combat before the judge, to be called upon to pay for his scuffed Rockport loafers.

Whether it be a physical combat, an adversarial conversation, a rational negotiation, or an exchange of visual cues and body language, you have appraised your adversary for what he is, a creature of sloth. As such his lack of discipline defines him.

He spits because he has no patience, no discipline; no self control. He is therefore easily influenced.

He smokes because he cannot handle stress, even the slightest stress. Furthermore, smoking has compromised his ability to handle stress once agitated, as his cardiovascular system is degraded. I have worked most of my life side-by-side with smokers, and have dated women who smoke. I have never met a smoker who can handle what I would consider moderate stress without 'cracking up'. Forget high stress. Just getting into an argument will push most of these people to the brink of aerobic and anaerobic failure.

I once survived a boxing session at the hands of a hyper-aggressive sparring partner, who was a smoker—not even a heavy smoker—without landing a punch. I threw plenty but he was a lot better than I. After a hundred or so unanswered punches, before I had even begun to bleed, he was coughing up brown goo on my shoes. Before taking up smoking this man had been a champion athlete. If you are a tough man, no cigarette smoker can put you away with his empty hands.

Whether your encounter with a slothful denizen of our social underbelly stays verbal or goes physical his sloth holds the key to your survival. Don't persecute the smokers. Let them proliferate. And then, when the Zombie Apocalypse comes, they will straggle and fall behind to be eaten alive, while you flee into the sunset on your healthy hindquarters, you disciplined little ape.

I Know That's Right!

Gorilla Wall Paul in the Ghetto

© 2012 James LaFond

This past Saturday, the 27th of October 2012, I called my West Baltimore ghetto connection, Big Gus, to get the skinny on the west side of the city. Gus is the big dude throwing me around the supermarket stockroom in the Logic of Force photos. I cringed when he mentioned Paul, the ill-fated janitor/parcel pickup guy who got stomped out by four Harm City hood rats behind the gorilla wall back at the end of winter this year [See Stoning Baboons]. But, when Gus told me that Paul was the viewpoint-smartass-social-commentator [my perennial gig] for this short tale, I glowed with biographical zeal as I took notes and grinned at the gathered slothful at the trash-covered bus stop...

Gus had been doing his chivalrous duty; looking in on Miss Ezz. Miss Ezz is a curvaceous HBI [Hebrew-by-Injection] who is of course in need of Big Gus' protection, particularly when 'The Man' is away at a manager's conference. Well, during the course of interviewing Miss Ezz, and making certain that she was safe, and free of all threats, Gus, highly trained security professional that he is, inquired as to the state of security outside, on the storefront, where Miss Ezz had just returned from her smoke break. Below is the brief tale she related to Gus. I thought that this little story offered a nice atmosphere piece, a look at the lighter side of Harm City strife...

Miss Ezz was sitting on the metal railing while the soft drink truck pulled up beside her at its regular time. It has been postulated by certain urban scholars that the soft-drink driver synchronizes his delivery to Cheap Guys are Us to coincide with Miss Ezz's appearance on the storefront. Paul, in charge of keeping the storefront tidy, happened to be sweeping around the shopping carts, oblivious to the reason for the soft-drink driver's leaning out the window or Big Gus' otherwise uncharacteristic security concerns.

Miss Ezz noticed that two denizens of the Hood were enjoying the Indian Summer sun; having set up a set of lawn chairs on the grass at the edge of the parking lot, as if this corner of the ghetto, scoured by windblown trash, were a Bahamian beach...

As Miss Ezz wondered at the odd vacation she was witnessing, a large heavyset middle-aged shoplifter burst out through the exit and lumbered by Paul. Looking up to see that the man was fleeing from the on duty uniformed Baltimore City police officer, Paul quipped at the footslogging shoplifter, "You betta run Fat Man!"

Then the heavyset middle-aged cop lumbered laboriously by Paul, and he quipped with a sneer, "You betta run fasta Fat Cop!"

Miss Ezz stood up besides Paul for a second or two, and then realized that 'The Man' would be wanting his inventory report soon, "Well Paul, let me get up in here. The Man sure knows how ta work a sista!"

Paul sagely commented, as he continued to sweep and critique the incompetent chase from a distance, "I know that's right Miss Ezz—I know that's right!"

If I were mayor, even if only for a day, Paul would be my spokesman.

Thanks Big Gus.

Narcostate News

I try and keep up with the blooming drug culture and the police state it enables in a regular column. Below are those entrees I thought book worthy.

Narco-State News #1

Tracking the Real Zombie Apocalypse

© 2013 James LaFond

Decades ago, in the degenerate 1970s, in the suburban hills of Western Pennsylvania, I was a lonely youth. I finally realized one day that my loneliness was due to drugs; specifically me not doing them. I remained defiant and did not join the rest of the student body in intoxication. I found two like-minded sober nerd souls and a repressed middle-aged woman to spend my time with. Not using drugs, more than anything, propelled me to drop out of school, go to work early, and begin a family at age 18. I could not imagine navigating the intoxicating haze of college that all of the middleclass suburban stoners fantasized about graduating to. I wanted to reach adulthood, and find that world where people thought clearly, where women would lay down with you without first having to get drunk or stoned.

The Real Zombie Apocalypse

Ten years later I found myself in Baltimore City, up to my neck in society-mandated debt, surrounded by drunken, drug-addicted and brain-damaged coworkers, criminals and bums. Twenty years after that I found myself in the same slum, with the ranks of the intoxicated swelled by my employers, the lowly employees I oversaw on their behalf, and police officers. Convinced now, that I had been more right than I could have imagined as a teenager; when I had viewed this nation as nothing but a human farming operation producing addicts to consume the drugs pushed by its masters; I decided to drop out, to find a small corner of sobriety in this stoned world and write.

My Harm City writing project is largely a study of a deeply intoxicated society. I relieve myself from this subject by reading and writing history and science-fiction, and by combat, where friends and I meet in a brutal attempt to carve a temporary niche of sanity, to escape from the chemically escaped addicts that surround us. A friend of mine is a doctor who confided that there is a type of doctor who he hates—and I think would like to execute en-masse—called a 'pain-management specialist'...just another pusher.

In light of all this one might excuse me for escaping America's twin unrealities of drugged oblivion and commercial delusion to the internet in search of news on something more sobering and brutally wide-eyed, like a good old-fashioned genocidal war in some mud-pit nation. 'Afghanistan' I thought, 'graveyard of empires, I'll read up on the slaughter and forget for many moments to come the zombie hordes of Baltimore...'

Stoner Wisdom

"Ten bucks for a ride man—ten bucks will get you anywhere 'cause it 'ill get me well...Shit brother, I miss being in prison. On the inside I can buy my shit with cigarettes. Out here I need cash ta get what I need..."

-Semaj

Stonernomics

Drugs and drug money in Baltimore are famously transported via trash bag. When the CIA sends money to Afghan drug lords how are these tens of millions of dollars delivered? Apparently suitcases, backpacks and plastic shopping bags are preferred.

Increase in Afghan heroin export under U. S. military occupation from 2001-2013: X40

Percentage of world heroin exported from U. S. occupied Afghanistan in 2013: 70-90%

-source, Nile Bowie, Malaysian-based political analyst

Annual income of Afghan drug lords: 700 million dollars

-source, Annie Machon, British MI5 defector

Heroin production as portion of Afghan GNP: 15%

Worldwide narcotics seizures at national borders: .02%

Internal narcotics seizures in U. S. and Europe: 10%

Legal penalty for possession of personal quantities of illegal drugs in Russia: 21 dollars

Drug profits laundered by leading world banks in the year 2008-2009: 352 billion dollars

-source, Russian Federal Drug Service

Gross National Product of Afghanistan: 6.96 billion dollars

-source, www.studentsoftheworld.info

I think those Afghan drug lords need to import some economic advisers from the West Baltimore housing projects and tweak that dreadful profit margin geometrically! I wonder if I'd get a cut of the consulting fee if I found Semaj and sent him over to Kandahar.

Narco-State News #2

Motown to Hotown

© 2013 James LaFond

I have known for a year that Detroit has the second highest murder rate in the U.S., the highest rate of abandoned houses, the largest population of feral dogs, and the world's only abandoned skyscraper. In fact, the History Channel's Life After People was filmed largely in Detroit. But there is more!

On July 11 2013 Detroit Free Press photographer Mandi Wright was arrested for filming an arrest, and held for 6 hours after her device was confiscated. [Sounds like dirty cops scrubbing video to me.]

-Source RT.com

Detroit cops only solve 10% of violent crimes.

Detroit police stations are typically only open from 8-12 hours per day.

Detroit has 11-times the murder rate of New York City.

50% of Detroit residents of employable age are unemployed.

47% of Detroit citizens are illiterate.

200 of 317 public parks in Detroit are closed!

-Source, financial analyst Patrick L. Young, living safely somewhere other than Hotown

This must be incorrect though. Because Our Dark Lord O'Sauran proclaimed just last year from Baradur on the Potomac, that he had saved Detroit. Perhaps he will have to send in some Nazgul drones to complete the job.

Elsewhere in the Narco-state...

The Las Vegas Rawlson-Neal Psyche Hospital discharged 1,500 patients, with 6 bottles of insure and three days' worth of anti-psychotics each, bought them one way bus tickets to various California cities, and launched them like a fleet of scud missiles at the People's Republic of California!

-Source, RT.com, 5/20/13

Police in Hawthorne, CA shot and killed a 52-year old man's pet dog and arrested him for filming a SWAT roadblock. Another bystander got it on film, escaped the Narco-state Thugs of the Hawthorne, CA Chapter, and uploaded it onto YouTube.

-Source, RT.com

Police in Mayfield Heights, Ohio are setting up fake drug checkpoints, and detaining and searching the vehicles of any motorist displaying suspicious behavior, like pulling over for directions.

-Source, Cleveland Plain-Dealer

Gothom Cops have reported the following race-based stats resulting from their 'stop and frisk' initiative targeting Hispanics and African Americans:

1 in 49 whites carry weapons

1 in 71 Hispanics carry weapons

1 in 93 African Americans carry weapons

[I'm wondering, since whites outnumber blacks and Hispanics combined, and we are far more likely to be armed, who do you really think is going to win the 'coming race war' that whites seem so worried about?]

1 in 43 whites carry drugs

1 in 57 Hispanics carry drugs

1 in 61 African Americans carry drugs [Of course, they just sold them to the white guys!]

-Source, RT.com 5/23/13

Hey Aunt Madeline, before you head up to Manhattan to catch that Broadway show, don't forget to leave your Tech-9 and that kilo of coke on the bus, okay.

Narco-state News #3

Planet Prozac

© 2013 James LaFond

Maybe it's just because I'm a nut, but it never occurred to me until recently that poor mental health might be a driver for addiction. I have generally been pretty callous where the addicted are concerned, pointing out how I beat my peanut M&M addiction to nicotine slaves for instance. My pet peeve is what I call the 'Instant family, just add alcohol' complex, personified by the occupants of stoner bars who have two drinks and then start calling you brother and hugging you.

This past weekend, I was reminded that my own mental health is often called into question by those around me. Brett and I had just finished a savage stick-fight when a female karate instructor asked me, "Where do you find all of these crazy people? I worked in mental health for fifteen years and never saw anything like this!"

I retorted, "That's because we have been hiding from you—beating each other in secret in basements and backrooms!"

Canadian Socrates to the Rescue

Stefan Molyneux is a philosopher I listen to on You—O'Sauron hasn't shut it down yet—Tube. He makes his living through donations, and I cannot afford to donate, so I promote him here. The following revelations are taken from a few of his recent podcasts. The comments in italics are my own callous opinion.

20-40% of young females are mentally ill, *depending on who is pointing the divining rod at them. Solomon Kane or Mohammad would have just burned the crazy woman, and Cochise would have moved his camp and left the angry bitch behind.*

1 in 4 women are on anti-depressants—*and the rest are smoking crack, shooting heroin, popping ills, sucking on cigarettes and knocking back booze.*

Traditional human cultures have 4 educators [mom, dad, grandma, granddad] to one student *[you, you little pain-in-the ass—the ballgame is on, get out of the way!]*

Currently, government schools in the developed world have 1 educator to 25 students, resulting in horizontal cultural conditioning [a mob mentality peer-pressure/consumer oriented mindset] or children raising children.

3 in 4 civilized children are struck or otherwise abused by their parents. *Come on Stefan, monkeys do it on Animal Planet, so it can't be our culture's fault.*

The unconscious mind processes information 7-8,000 times faster than the conscious mind. *This is why intuition and dreams were traditionally trusted by early man, and why less analytic-dependent women seem to be so good at picking out a loser at a glance, and maybe get depressed easier than their male counterparts who are still trying to quantify the cultural decay around them.*

95% of people have a conscience, and are hence potentially well-meaning.

4% of people have no conscience and see people as nothing but tools to be manipulated. Politicians are naturally drawn from this segment of humanity. These are the creeps who manipulate the majority of the 95-percentile into doing bad things to one another in the guise of some perceived good cause. *Military history would be pretty boring without these people. Do not threaten the quality of my nonfiction reading list Stefan!*

1% of people have an anti-conscience and mean to harm others for the sake of enjoying the infliction of said negative action.

Since 1998 psychopathy has doubled

Have a nice day with your crazy lady of choice, and remember to thank Stefan from Free Domain Radio for the disturbing diagnosis of your matrimonial bliss.

I, for one, am feeling depressed just now—where is my stick?

Narco State News #4

Junky Cognate

© 2013 James LaFond

Every day junkies, crack-heads, dope-fiends and drunks continue to amaze me, as I watch them at bus stops sucking on their one shared addiction, the cigarette. More and more they recede into my mind's eye as an alien species, some un-consumable prey animal, perhaps an invasive species like a stink bug. What is more they are reproducing.

Last night I was on a 10:45 bus when two late night regulars got on, with one of their four small children—the infant. I can only hope that the other three, who generally supervise themselves, were in better care. But really, what is the point? They are doomed with parents like this. The 25-year-old father is a grungy little dude with a cigarette perpetually behind his ear. He carries a heavy backpack, and wheels two strollers, a large one loaded with groceries, the other a small model loaded with their tiny red-headed baby. The mother is a tall heroin addict, incapable of holding the baby, forever nodding out. She appears to be knocked up again. Their ponderous presence on the bus is always an irritant. They are, by the way, subsidized by your tax dollars, hauling enormous loads of groceries on food stamp week.

This morning I was standing at a bus stop where three people were gunned down this past winter, a half mile from the scene of a home-invasion/double-shooting three nights ago. I was standing off, avoiding the cigarette smoke. A cop was idling at the traffic stop. A drug dealer was dispensing 'perks' and 'oxys', to some middle-aged dope-fiends, folding his bills neatly, making change like a seasoned carnival hand.

Related Trivia

The fastest growing crime in Europe is 'metal theft'. This is the surest sign of a growing population of drug addicts. In Portugal farmers are forming militias to guard irrigation valves.

California State handles about 150,000 prisoners per year, farming out about 20,000 of these inmates to Correction Corporation of America [215 million per year] and GEO Group [150 million per year]. The state's unholy prison guard union, the CCPOA, has bribed Governor Brown with one check for $196,770 and, before him, The Governator with $22,300. The State prison budget is around 8 billion.

Nationwide, prison corporations are awarded contracts that guarantee 90% to 100% occupancy! Think about that.

If you think that is bad, consider that it costs New York City $167,731 per year to house an inmate! It would be cheaper to send these guys to Yale—and a lot more fun too!

Red Tee

Nightfall in the Narcostate

© 2014 James LaFond

Yesterday afternoon, Saturday, 1/25/14, I went shopping at Fort Hoodrat. I acquired my food, an unusual haul of $33.87 worth of discounted chow that should last me two weeks. This failure to resist a good deal or ten resulting in my breaking one of the cardinal rules of urban awareness I have preached on this site and in numerous books: people on foot who are 'burdened' with packages, or anything that occupies their attention and/or both of their hands, have their risk of attack increased geometrically.

There I was, walking through my favorite 2.5 foot wide alley from an ice-covered back lot to the main drag, when I thought to myself, 'Wow, if only I were drunk, or at least buzzed, I would be the perfect crime victim!'

Narco Night Train

Inspired, I emerged onto the main drag next to the bar which, in 2013, beneficently supplied a half dozen mugging victims to the kids that get their hair cut at the barber shop next door, and instead of turning left for home, turned right and entered the bar. Fortunately for my experiment, and my thin wallet, my alcohol tolerance is low.

Two hours and four cheap drafts later, as darkness fell, I checked my pen, my razor, my keys, and tied off the bags of groceries in case I needed to use them as flails, and walked out into a young icy cold night.

The traffic was more sparse than summer, spring or Autumn. There was almost no one on foot. As I am rarely approached even during prime hunting season I had slim hopes of being attacked and writing my 'I rumbled in the hood over ten cans of corned beef hash' masterpiece. Never-the-less I forged on up the road toward the ATM where so many were tailed from to the point of their mugging last year.

As I neared the ATM and the hipster babe that was using it, a tall, thin, sallow-faced whitetrashian with coal black hair approached me, "Hey man, do you know where the AA meeting is?"

I stepped off and glared at him.

He said, "Please man, I live in the halfway house next to the crackhouse [50 yards off] and was supposed to go with my roommates and they left me. I need to make that meeting man."

I stepped forward and kept eye-contact, my packages still in my hands. I don't talk to people on the street unless it is a woman, an elder, or a handicapped person. The guy was beginning to tear up, "Please man, where's the church with the AA meeting."

I did not know, did not care, and would not have told him if I did know.

I began to walk off and the babe from the ATM machine, with a disgusted glance at me, stepped up and said, "It's right in the basement of the church almost to Northern parkway."

He said, "Thank you miss," and hurried up the road.

She glared at me, "You heartless bastard!"

I walked on and crossed the street to the Pakaistani gas station where the crackheads buy their crack, the crack-hos buy their condoms, and I buy my weekly dark Milkyway bar. As I checked my bags outside the door before continuing home, a mixed-raced teenager who appeared to be mentally handicapped, stepped up to me, with his hands in his hooded coat and began to mumble, with wide tear-filled eyes, "Red-tee, doubleyou cap, red-tee—got you red-tee."

I looked at him in disbelief, "What?"

He blinked that kind of wide-eyed blink that someone uses to get sand out of their eyes, "I got you red-cap, doubleyou cap—can get some yellow-cap."

I just shook my head, now realizing that I was the subject of a drug marketing campaign that used retarded children to make sales like used car dealerships used former high school athletes.

I then grinned and he asked innocently, as if I had landed from some alien planet where white people did not get stoned, "You don't get high?!?"

I shook my dead 'no'.

He continued, "You don't do dope?"

I shook my head 'no'.

He made a last ditch attempt, "Do you wanna try?"

Not having quite the cruel streak necessary to abuse the retarded, I just walked off, and this kid followed me, his hands still in his pockets. I looked over my shoulder, noticing that he was shorter and stronger than I, and that we walked on an icy sidewalk that contrasted in a glistening manner to the salt-bleached asphalt beyond.

I stepped aside and let him pass. I gave him a one block lead assuming he was headed up the street to the stoner bar to unload his goods. Then he turned up my street. It is so rare for anyone to walk a distance that, if I am ever being followed by a person who turns down the same side street as I do, I give it a half block, or until the first cover, and then turn on them. I once did this with a guy I was convinced was going to hit me for Baltimore Area Skin Heads. When I could tell by the look in his eyes that he had no idea why I was trying to stab him in the neck with a nail I had just plucked out of the gutter, I backed off.

I am so glad I let this kid pass, because, not only did he not mean to do me harm, but he is a neighbor. I live within 100 yards of a group home [criminals on probation], a halfway house [drunks & dopefiends on the court-mandated mend], and a flop house. This kid apparently lives in and/or works out of, the flop house, two doors up from where I sit typing. He entered the apartment occupied by Binky, the only resident of that atrocious excuse for bad 1920s architecture who owns a car, a real nice car.

Welcome to the neighborhood kid.

Narcostate News #5

'White Kills 10 Baltimore Junkies'

© 2014 James LaFond

No, Randy Bracken is not on the loose in Baltimore. The 'white' that is killing these dopefiends , and 27 of their brethren statewide, is a 'super white' mixture of heroin and fentanyl cooked up on the Left Coast and shipped east. Federal, state and local police, as well as bleeding heart junkie support organizations, are in a panic over this loss of their client base. What would law enforcement do In the U.S. if all of the dopefiends suddenly died?

The Sun Paper reporters who broke the news here did tout the fact that Baltimore heroin addicts would not let something like this slide by because they are 'educated' 'savvy customers', and that the dead are probably recent converts from the oxycontin market.

As a Darwinist I really have no problem with overdose deaths. I stood in two different Baltimore area public restrooms on different occasions and watched junkies die. It, did, not, bother, me. These people are dying doing what they love, what they live for. It would be like me dying from a stick fight, or from a massive heart attack induced by a night with Jennifer Lopez'.

Tattoo Rick always said that the cure for the drug epidemic was to pile the dope up on the side of the road and let all of the losers do their imitation of Scarface snorting a mountain.

I second the motion.

Sam Yo

On Getting Got

© 2014 James LaFond

At 12:15 this past Sunday afternoon I approached a Harm City bus stop where a young hoodlum was ranting and raving to an older couple who were headed home from church. When I stepped up he, seeming to find me a more likely repository for his indignation, stepped over to me to plead his case. I was minus a notepad, so I recorded Sam's trials and tribulations in the back of the book I was reading, Jack Donavan's The Way of Men.

"Yo, he god me. I shoulda knowd it was like that. I put da fitty in' is hand and he put da bag in my pocket. He tellin' me he god da diesel, dat he got dat diesel shit. He god me good. Den I smell dat shit and it stink. You know whad it was; it was dat oregano shit: you know dat fake-ass shit you sprinkle on you food; that shit!

"Bitch-ass nigga! And was a black nigga, not no white nigga or no other kind a nigga. Shit, black niggas aint for each other they for dat monay. Bitch-ass nigga—I gonna smoke dat nigga! I'm gonna smoke dat bitch-ass nigga!"

Never fear Sam, this white-ass nigga feels for you, having been duped by a preserver of the oldest stoner rip-off ruse in the book.

Heinous Huffers

The Most Despicable Dopefiends

© 2014 James LaFond

Last Wednesday night during the recent blizzard I made it to work at Fred's Fine Foods For Foodstampers just before midnight. I work the frozen foods and dairy case over night. The place was trashed. What was glaringly apparent was that the whipped topping section in the dairy was empty. There were only a few cans left. The night captain was walking by and I pointed at the empty shelf, "Do we have a surge in bachelorette parties around here."

He shook his head in disgust and set down three cans of the aerosol dairy cream and groused, "The drug dealers must be snowed in. All of the druggies are walking out with this stuff."

An hour later after I stocked the section two snot-nosed punks, pasty white and pimpled, and doing a piss poor job of representing the Caucasian gene pool, came through the aisle and headed back to the bathroom. While I was stacking my empty pallets these two headed up front. A minute later Ron came back with an armful of Readywhip and handed it to me, "I told the dummies if they didn't cough it up I was calling the police, so I didn't have to chase them. As stupid as they are the last thing they need is to be snorting more of this stuff."

Huffing aerosol is predominantly a passion of white teenagers, although, in later years many will fall back on it in lean times long after they have moved on to better drugs. When I worked in South Baltimore I had to check the aerosol whip before I touched it. Down there those fends would unzip the seal and blast all of the gas up their nose right there in the aisle, resulting in nose bleeds. Most nights that I worked at the Fort Avenue store I had at least one canister on the dairy shelf with blood and other nasal secretions dripping down the side.

This was also a habit in Northeast Baltimore stores. I once worked with a crew who all huffed the Airwick room freshener and then sat back against the pallet stack and giggled and said "Wow man" for an hour.

South Baltimore was the worst. There were three
particular boys who had stomped an older black
dishwasher to death a month before I began
working in the neighborhood. My new coworkers
told me to be careful walking on Key Highway
coming in because these guys were notorious, their
Uncle was politically connected, and everyone in
the area 'knew' they had killed the man, but they
had not even been arrested. I thought the stories of
the murder seemed a bit over blown, and did not
imagine the cops being that incompetent.

Then one night, while I was stocking the ice cream
with my back to the Readywhip case, these three
came in behind me and starting huffing gas. When
the security guard said something to them they
started bragging about having beaten a man to
death. If I said anything it would have ended badly.
The lead kid was short and potbellied. I turned to
put my plastic in the trash box and accidently
shoulder butted him in the chin. They all got quiet
while I stared in his face. I was holding a large
utility knife in my right hand. I told the security
man that I needed to get a cart from out front and
would be walking up with him. The three punks
walked between us chuckling, mumbling and acting
tough, until they got to the checkout. The security

guard put the canisters on the belt so they could pay for their huff, and out the door they went, without a fuss.

I hope one night I get to see one of these fiends literally blow his brains out with this stuff. I'll gladly swing the mop that erases his stain.

'Junkie Juice in Aisle Nine'

A Survey Of Subhuman Stains in Harm City Eateries and Food Markets

© 2014 James LaFond

"Please Lord don't let me die in a supermarket!"

-Miss Ezz

Last night I was breaking down three dairy pallets in the stockroom, when a local heroin dealer and a junkie walked through to the bathroom. This dealer uses the men's room at Free Food For Fat F...s to sell dope to people that need help firing up.

The dealer is a forty-year old black man who constantly mumbles cusswords. It is as if Richard Pryor was drunk, angry and stumbling around trying to memorize his jokes. I think this dude does this to project an air of menace and to keep people away. His junkie was an emaciated white boy of perhaps 20. They came through mumbling and cussing to no one in particular at 12:05.

Three employees attempted to access the two toilet men's room over the course of the next half hour. By 12:30 the dealer was gone, cussing furiously to himself as he walked by me. Finally Zach tried to use the urinal and came back out in disgust, asking me how long the junkie had been there. I responded, "He must be having a hard time. The guy that helped him fire up just left in disgust. With any luck the coroner will be carting him off under a sheet in a few hours."

Zach grabbed the night captain, who spent the next 10 minutes watching the bathroom drama. By the time I was out on the floor with my freight at 12:40 the junkie was staggering around the store. The night captain spent the next hour as the personal security guard and safety manager for the stoned junkie, who never ended up buying a thing.

Junkies in Winter

About 15 years ago a KFC I used to walk by was closed down after a body was found to have been in the men's room for 2 days.

The same year I saw a junkie overdose in the men's room of a supermarket I worked in.

In December Scabby Abby was caught shooting heroin in the women's room at Wal-Mart.

Earlier this winter a junkie was found dead in a Burger King close to where I live, having been draining in the bathroom for an entire day.

Last Friday, at the local Dunkin Doughnuts a junkie overdosed in the men's room, and was revived by the cops and EMTs.

This past Sunday Miss Ezz, bookkeeper at Cheap Guys R Us in West Baltimore, called me.

"You would not believe what I've had to put up with this week with these ghetto cashiers and these drug dealer customers. We sell fifty cases of garlic powder a week [25 times normal]. The drug dealers put it in their coke and heroin to throw off the police dogs. Then, on Saturday night this junkie dies in the men's room, a needle sticking out of his arm. Nobody missed a beat. The EMTs came and tried to revive him. The cops came and taped off the area. The CSI people and the coroner come. They eventually wheel the body out, and we keep pumping out the groceries; customers pushing their shopping carts of sodas and oodles of noodles around the corpse on the gurney. Nobody even blinked. Please don't let me die in one of these places—please!

"Then I have to use the woman's room—a regular pit of filth; women pissing on the walls—how does someone without a dick piss on the wall? The generals [janitors] sign the bathroom log, but they just take a dirty mop and push the germs around. It is bad enough that I have to use this room, then I get inside and the light does not work. The first thing I think is I might be tripping over a body! I had to prop the door open with the trash can to let in enough light—someone should just condemn the neighborhood."

I would like to recommend needle exchange stations at the entrance to supermarket restrooms, a Pink Floyd music feed in the men's room, as well as crime tape and a body bag in the janitorial closet. Bleeding hearts feel free to improvise your own Junkie aid station. In the meantime bring on the China White.

Crack Hos & Heroin Honeys

One Night in a Supermarket Restroom

© 2014 James LaFond

Last night, 4/11/14, I arrived at Free Food for Fat F…s at 11:27. As I approached the store front I noticed one bum sleeping on the sidewalk, one stoner twitching and rocking on the curb, and one crack head pacing before the front door, hassling the two customers ahead of me about something. As I entered the fool tried to block my progress and I shouldered by him and he said, "Sir? Sir?? Sir???"

After his pleas for whatever he wasn't going to get went unanswered three times he followed me a few steps and said, "I hate it when you people act all retarded. Can't you people hear what I'm saying?"

All of those fools were white, a demonstrable display of what Anglo-American culture has become in Drug War America.

I noticed, when I passed by the women's room to get to my refrigerated storage areas to begin processing the dairy order out in the stockroom, that the door to that facility did not close. Over the course of the next three hours I was back and forth through this hallway often. Something was the matter with the hinge. I had a large order, and a frozen order also, so did not take out time to jot down the times of the following occurrences. I can, however, give approximate times.

12:00 a.m.: A worn out old crack-ho—an emaciated bleach-blonde with cadaverous skin stretched over poorly formed bones—was smashing a rock of crack up on the women's room sink and snorting it. She would then cough up a wad of oral secretions, launch it onto the floor, and smash another rock, which she would then snort with all of the grace of my mother's old dust-buster. She walked past me with a mumbled 'goodnight' as she left through the stockroom.

12:30 a.m.: A fat white woman and a scrawny black dude went back into the women's room and smoked a hit of crack cocaine. They were all business, in and out in ten minutes.

1:30 a.m.: Two soaking wet white trash hos of hoggish proportions, wearing spandex and heavy makeup, ho hoop earrings dangling from their pale beefy lobes, were escorted past me by a small black man of extremely dark complexion and smiling continence. He is a drug dealer who has used our facility before and he cheers up and says, "Hey Yo" as he herds his heifers on by. They all three repair to the two stall women's room. I do not know what transpired in the plush accommodations as I went up front for my coffee break. Fifteen minutes later, as I sat on the bench at the front door, they walked out through the register lane without making a purchase, laughing and giggling all the way. He flashed an ivory smile at me and escorted his portly harem out the door.

2:30 a.m.: Officer Manfriendly, my personal oppressor, walked in to use the men's room in his paramilitary getup. As I inventory his Batman utility belt it occurs to me that the women's room is definitely the place to fire dope and smoke crack.

3:00 a.m.: A very attractive couple enters and begins shopping with a basket. She is tall, elegant, and white, not busty enough to pose in playboy, and not thin enough to model clothes. She is beautiful in the very high heels she can barely stand on, doing the dopefiend lean as she is. Her date is a short muscular black man with his pants actually buckled around his waist. They are in their late twenties and he can't keep his hands off of her as she staggers and drools in the aisle. He has a powder blue hat. She carries a finely stitched black leather purse about the size of one of her shoes. They cannot decide who should be pushing the cart. They head back to the women's room and have sex standing up, between the stall doors and the sink, with the door wide open. She is bent over the sink and he is having a hard time getting his pelvis level with her rather remarkable Caucasian ass. She is spreading her legs to get lower for him. When I pass again coming back from the cooler he has had the decency to push her up against the wall so that she is not exposed to passersby. After their ten minute tryst they shop for another 20 minutes and then leave hand-in-hand.

3:30 a.m.: The frozen food man is walking in the front door. I am taking my lunch up on the bench waiting for him. We sort the frozen order together on Saturday mornings. He is being followed by a fifty year old crack head who asks him for a ride to his house no less than nine times, which is how many times I counted the question. In between each request for a lift Rob says the following, sometimes repeating his answer after the next repetition of the plea for a 'lift man':

"No man, no."

"I'm not losing my job to give you a lift dude."

"Hey asshole, how many ways do I have to say no?"

"Get lost you loser!"

"Ask him [the night captain] to call a cab for you."

"Get the fuck away from me man!"

"You're a sentence away from losing the rest of your teeth pal!"

I punched in with Rob as the night captain called a cab for the crack-head, who then disappeared into the night like a phantom, not wanting a cab at all. When we got back to the walk-in freezer around the corner from the restroom he went on a rant, "What a trashy neighborhood this is. I was in a good mood, now I'm all torqued up over that loser. What has happened to the white race? They're worse than the niggers!"

I responded, "Then you'll be glad to know that they aren't reproducing. All the white dudes come in stoned or drunk, and alone. The white girls come in stoned or drunk with sober black dudes. According to the sexual activity in the women's room there the trash of the future is going to be brown."

He grabs the ice cream rack and looks at me in dismay, "Can you imagine how stupid that generation 'ill be!"

Spring is sprung and all is sloth out in the Narcostate.

The Ghetto Grocer, over and out.

Harm City Seat Beat

How One Drug Wholesaler Uses Police For Muscle

© 2014 James LaFond

This past week I was walking buy a storefront business in a part of Harm City that I will not discuss. Nor will I discuss the name or nature of the business, because I want to live!

This store front is on a primary street, in Baltimore City. It is a retail outlet which legitimately sells electronic devices. It is also a major narcotics outlet with the local dealers drawing most of their product from this one source. This is not the actual stash house but the contact point.

Knowing this, I was quite surprised to see a uniformed Harm City cop, sitting in the store on a chair provided for his use while he played video games on a handheld electronic device. The owner stood beside him, glaring at some young hoodlums across the street.

I went next door and bought two beers, which netted me two sources of information. Apparently, this drug wholesaler had his legit retail business robbed by a pair of young thugs. Even as he is arranging for the professional level disposal of these hoodlums, he must also arrange for the protection of his business. There is a Baltimore City program by which retail business operators may pay the police department the overtime rate for one of its police officers. This costs no more than a good armed security guard and acts as a much better deterrent, because every criminal knows that if you hurt or kill a cop you are toast.

So, even as word goes out that King Blo needs some muscle to settle a score, King Blo himself stands besides his very own pet cop, playing Angry Birds on his smart phone. I find this to be all very interesting, and surprisingly practical.

'Five-O Yo?'

'Is You Serious?': The Rise of Vanilla Fudge

© 2014 James LaFond

Yesterday afternoon I went down onto the main drag to watch the police in action. A group of black teens and a mixed race trio we are calling 'Vanilla Fudge' after the type of Oreo cookie that has fudge filling and two white crackers, have been terrorizing the local businesses. In fact, even though there were cops out in force, these guys were still jacking the merchants, right under their noses.

For the third time this week one electronics merchant was robbed by Vanilla Fudge. The local business owners are looking into gun permits. The word has come down from a local politician for the cops to 'make a show of force' in this partially re-gentrified neighborhood. The crime has gotten so bad that the non-violent criminals are helping. A vigilante sentiment is rising as the crime is beginning to look like a guerilla war waged by a handful of young men and boys against the entire neighborhood. Below is a chronology of how the depredations of Vanilla Fudge and the 'punk-ass stickup boys' effected the evening's festivities.

5/31/14, 5 to 10 p.m.

1. A crack ho knocks back vodka and Mountain Dew on the sidewalk as she rattles off a description to a cop. The cop ignores the open container violation.

2. A heroin addict who was just robbed by a teenage punk tells her brothers and they beat him badly. This is going on in a back lot while the cops are working the street on the other side of the brownstone business strip. The cops decline to investigate their vigilante actions.

3. When Vanilla Fudge rob a drug wholesaler's front business—again—a young 'customer' of his volunteers to ride along with the cops and point out Vanilla Small. Within a half hour Vanilla Small is cuffed on the curb awaiting the paddy wagon.

4. The entire neighborhood is now on the lookout for Vanilla Big and Fudge.

5. I begin drinking cheap beer in a dive bar and two young ladies, worried about being robbed and claiming to admire my arms and tactfully declining

to mention my equally well-developed gut, ask me to walk them home. I agree to walk them home to a loft apartment at the top of what was once a suburban mansion in a different age. They leave to go buy the food they plan on cooking for me, and I stay behind to drink one more beer, feeling like Edward Woodward in The Wicker Man.

6. Way, the local upscale drug dealer, who conducts business at the bar on his smart phone, comes in with a date. The last time I spoke to Way he asked me what I was writing. At the time I was writing 'The Pussy Trap', a chapter in Taboo You. He looked up at me and said most sagely, with a self-defeated tone, "Oh that is a deep trap!" Now I see just how deep Way's pussy trap is, as he walks in with a babe that could be a cover girl for King Magazine, draped in silk, bangled in gold, and possessed of more curves than a Formula One course. He gives her money to play pool so he can 'conduct bidness' while every other man in the bar gawks open-mouthed at her bending over the table. Then two cops walk in! Way looks up in disbelief, looking as if he just saw some sewage at the base of his Corona, "Five-O Yo? Is you serious Yo? Oh, this shit has gone too far! A dude cain't even take care a his bidness 'cause a punk-ass stick-up boys!" the cops hang out

and drink water, talking to the patrons amicably as Way groans and rolls his eyes, phone now in his pocket.

7. I finish my beer and meet the ladies at the market to escort them home. I discover that they have a six-pack of beer for me and begin to think that maybe I am the unforeseen beneficiary of the Vanilla Fudge rampage. I get the ladies safely home and sit out above the weird Baltimore skyline that seems like a West Virginia townscape from this vantage. I'm getting really drunk while they cook indoors, and decide that I need to make my escape before beer six, or I might not get home with my discretion intact.

8. Two hours later, having been fed a meal that could have nourished a third world village for a week, so drunk that I can count my heartbeats in my ears, and armed with a very ergonomic bottle of cheap merlot, I make my way home through the back alleys, back lots, and across the largely forsaken catholic church grounds of Hamilton Baltimore, wondering if my keyboard will respect me in the morning.

Thanks Vanilla Fudge. Oh, a heads up, steer clear of Way en his 'fo real nigga'. Your entrepreneurial efforts remain woefully underappreciated.

Narco Night Train

Smoking History

Notes On Editing The Past

© 2014 James LaFond

The other night I saw a lame WWII movie, which failed to keep me awake. One thing that did strike me was the notice that it was rated PG-13 for 'historical smoking'!

Are you kidding me!

How ridiculous. Keep in mind that I hate cigarettes, am allergic to them, hate cigarette smokers, and have written the blood spattered novelette Menthol Rampage in which a man with my condition goes postal and kills smokers in a mania to be avenged upon their vile selves as often as possible before the cops put him down.

I have been horrified at how many young people smoke. However, it is none of my business unless they blow it in my face. I recently watched The Day the Earth Stood Still from 1952 in which doctors were pictured smoking in an examination room and an entire family was smoking at breakfast! I thought it was hilarious, and, it should be rated G. Our children and grandchildren should have every opportunity to see how ridiculously stupid, rude and vile their great grandparents' generation was.

Excuse me, but we have known since the stone age, when we smoked those obsolete hominids from their dens 100,000 years ago, that smoke inhalation kills reliably.

Look, if myself and the last nine other humans on earth were rescued by aliens right before Allah's Comet hit, and those nine people smoked, and were provided with unlimited tobacco by the aliens, I would be the last member of my species on the second day out from earth.

Making cigarettes taboo is nothing more than a guarantee that our youth will smoke for defiance's sake. This is what we get for winning WWII. The brats born to the Greatest Generation now sandblast our minds at every opportunity. I should not complain though, for I now have a hope, a reason to live into old age. I want to live long enough to see an America where the busybody descendents of the pilgrims no longer set the cultural bar; an America overrun by polite Asians and Hispanics who could care less what we watch or think.

The White Vice Lords

Harm City Opens It's Unclean Arms

© 2014 James LaFond

I have noticed a recent spike in violent crimes in my neighborhood, with an increase in participation by young hip-hop identified white males. Two weeks ago I took the bus with one of the most vicious looking young whites I have seen in quite a while—you know, these white people can get scary when they forget they represent those other white people who own everything.

As are 8 out of 10 people under 30 this man is heavily tattooed. He is fit. He has hard facial lines without trying, definitely the product of negative socialization. He is blonde, a tough looking middleweight I would say. He has three teardrops tattooed below the outside of his left eye.

I ran into a young lady in her twenties by the food market who is very pregnant, and who I have carried groceries for. She seemed very nervous about getting home before dark. I asked her why.

"You know it's a rough area. Up on Bayonne we have three crack houses and a heroin den. They are all over the place. But now I have these three guys that just came in from out of town living on my street, three doors down. They are beating the shit out of people and just taking their stuff. I saw them jack this one guy that was walking with his wife. The guy was older. This dude with the teardrops walks up to him and cracks him hard to the ground—takes his phone, empties his pockets. In the street, during the day!

"Nobody is calling the cops because they know these guys will be around when the cops aren't. The cops can't protect you. What are you going to do, file a complaint, so the cop can give these dudes you're name and address like you're going to the people's Court to argue over back rent? I don't think so.

"Anyways, they're getting popular. They have girls over their every night—whores, drug-heads and ghetto bitches, stripping down to the waist and throwing hands in the street like they're filming a ghetto brawl video for YouTube. I stay clear of them. What's scary is I'm sure they're more coming'. These guys call themselves the 'Vice Lords'. These are hard dudes to be coming in white and forming up in an area like this where you have all of this established black shit goin' on.

"I'm really afraid about staying around once my baby comes. These guys scare me. They're startin' shit with the other drug houses, taking their girls. It could get bad."

I had thought the Vice Lords was a black gang based in Chicago. I don't know if these guys are affiliates or not. I've never been any good at reading gang tags, of which we have had an increase over the past 18 months. I suppose it's about time I get started.

A Conversation between Zombies

On The Bus to Purgatory with Two Arguments for White Genocide

© 2014 James LaFond

Thursday 7/10/14, 8:34 a.m.

It is not a proud day to be a white man in Harm City. I sit on a bus full of black working people going to and fro their shitty jobs in their company polo shirts. Then two of my people get on. This is a cross town bus, which means it always has stoners on board. You see drug-addicted drunks spend their entire lives shuttling between the hospitals, courts, police stations, and rehab clinics that are the focal points of the city bus routes. Drunken brawls, stoned falls, pavement arrests for possession— really, how many knees in the back can one dope-fiend take before he has to up his pain killer intake?—make these guys as beat up at 40 as a 1970s NFL player.

To everyone's dread the inevitable conversation starts. I will not spell this the way it sounded, as that would be irritating to some readers who have a hard time with slang dialogue in print. Suffice it to say that a cigarette smoking, pot-smoking, pill-popping, crack-smoking, smack-firing alcoholic sounds like a 70 year old deaf, downs' syndrome sufferer. They speak loud, double up on all vowels, and repeat themselves between three and five times. I will also not loop the dialogue. Just know that I listened to the following conversation for 25 minutes. Imagine taking 25 minutes to say this:

Stoner Fool [SF]: "Fuck man! Fuck!"

Stoner Genius [SG]: "What man? What!"

SF: "My leg man, my leg!"

SG: "I thought the doc fixed it."

SF: "He put me in a space suit man. I said, 'What the fuck doc?' en he says, 'What da fuck what?' So I'm like look maaann [sorry, I could not resist] I'm not goin' to no outer space, so why the fuck am I in a space suit?'"

SG: "So man, what did he say?"

SF: "He said he put all kind a metal junk in there man, holding my leg together, so I have the space boot."

SG: "I thought they had you in the suit."

SF: "No man, just a factor of speech. I just had the boot. But this bigass boot might as well have been the whole suit—like how am I gonna defend myself with this fuckin' boot man. Last time I was casted up dudes fuckin' mugged me man. Slapping this fuzzy shit on you is like putting a 'fuck with me' sign on my back man! Fuckin' docs man—nails in my fickin' leg, holdin' my fuckin' bones in place! Fuck!"

Keep in mind that these guys are so loud that no one else on the bus can even have a conversation without shouting, so we all remain silent listening to these two.

SG: "Man, that shit ain't nails—it's screws man."

SF: "I know I'm screwed man. You don't have to fuckin' rub it in!"

SG: "I ain't rubbin' shit man. I said, those are screws—had my own leg bolted together before from that fuckin' pig down in Highland Town."

SF: "Man, I said I know I'm screwed, and I would have bolted if I a knowed he was a fuckin' narc! Pig did not identify him self! I am suin' that fucker, suin' the whole city! These nails in my leg are killing me and my old lady's son snagged my Oxy's."

SG: "Look, they don't put nails in your leg man."

SF: "It's metal man—so it's a fuckin' nail! It hurts, so it's a fuckin' nail! Ain't wherein' that fuckin' space boot man—God this shit hurts—fuckin' nails in my leg."

SG: "Hey man, remember the time we stomped the shit out of that dude down in Pig Town for fuckin' with our shit!"

SF: "Yeah man, what's his face. Can't do that shit with a space boot and nails in your leg man!"

I offloaded from that bus at this point in the conversation three hours ago. I have to believe, that somewhere that conversation is still ongoing.

'Snitches Get Stitches'

A Doper's View of the Police State

© 2014 James LaFond

The following is an interview with Sal the hacker about his days as a 'doper'.

I always worked, usually construction. When I had no work I would hack to get my money.

Yeah, I was a doper, but I never dealt. I worked, I hacked, I bought my shit, and I did my shit. I didn't like the drug scene—the hanging out part. I just needed my shit. I was major ADHD in school. It was a fight to get me to school every day. I hated sitting still; wanted to play, to work with my hands. They pumped me full of school drugs until I was old enough to get signed out. So, for my twenties and into my thirties I pumped myself full of my own shit to keep level.

One time I'm hacking, over on Route 40 driving this dude to one of his houses. A guy will supply more than one house. This dude uses buses, cabs and hacks to get around. An army of cops pull up and I have five of them dragging me out of my car; spread eagle on the asphalt, my elbows and knees getting skinned, my face in the gravel, a knee in the back of my neck and a gun against the upside of my face.

These cops are screaming at me for being a piece of shit. Some of these cops are my regulars who took half of whatever dope they found on me and let me go on my way. But when their bosses decide to grab you that tax don't hold. Of course if you snitch on a cop, well then you're either in prison for life or dead. There are only so many places you can go to get your shit. The cops know all of them. They'll catch you coming out and either arrest you with a lifetime worth of trumped up charges or shoot you dead.

A dead doper?

Nobody gives a shot about that.

They take me in for interrogation, beating my ass and screaming in my face for five hours. They want to know where this guy's houses are. They want to know about other suppliers. They want me to commit suicide.

I tell them, "Look, I'm a doper. I get my shit from a dozen different guys on street corners, and I get gone. I don't deal. I don't snitch. Snitches get stitches and then they die. You guys have to be crazy if you think I'm snitching."

After five hours they let me go. Of course the car is impounded although I have done nothing but give a dude a ride who did not even have any dope on him—they found nothing on him. I don't have the impound fee, so I lose the car and can't hack anymore. Some fuckin' cop probably got my car for change at auction, and now I'm on bus stops.

It's better than dead.

Roderick's Plight

'I Survived the Nineteen-Sixties for This?'

© 2014 James LaFond

Roderick is a small retired black man in his mid 60s who attends Baltimore City Community College and a Baltimore County martial arts school where I train and coach. We see each other twice a month and every month he has at least one tale to tell of a black youth or youths threatening, challenging, extorting or attacking him. Here is Roderick's life of retired adventure for the first week of September 2014.

"I have been practicing what you have told me, about the entire game being about not letting the situation go physical, even if it means humiliation."

When Roderick came up being a black man in Baltimore was like being a member of a warrior tribe and meant fighting whenever you were attacked or threatened. A 'brutha' who did not fight back could

*expect no support from others and faced an
increased likelihood of attack.*

"Especially, since back in the day I have some
assault charges for when I defended myself. I know
the judge will just see that and his eyes will glaze
over. These young hoodlums, if they got no record
yet, will walk, and I'll be doin' time at my age, for
defendin' myself."

"Lately it has not been the teenage boys but dudes
in their early twenties. You know I thought that one
day that when I became a senior citizen people
would respect that and leave me alone. I did not
bank on having to come here and train to fight for
my life on the street in my sixties!"

"I live down in the City, Charles Village. I use the
Bank of America. You would think it would be safe
to use the ATM on a busy street corner around the
way from the police precinct where there cameras
and dozens of dudes just hanging out—the
homeless type of dudes.

"I go to the ATM and take out my money—mind you
it's not just twenty bucks, but over a hundred.
Before I even step away this young dude walks up
to me and says, "He old man, I need a few dollars."

I'm standin' there with my life in my hands, my rent money, a roof over my head, and this thug is steppin' to me wantin' money, knowin' that all I got is twenties.

"I said, 'What?'"

"He says, 'I need some money.'"

"That's when I knew this wasn't panhandlin'. It was stupidity or something worse. I said, 'Get away!' and I stepped off. Then he goes over to this gigantic young dude—a huge monster baby with no brains—and whispers somethin' to him, and that big baby flexes all angry. Then you know what's up. They marking me man. I can't use that ATM no more."

"So now, today, I need to get my money, so come out to the Bank of America out here, where, you know, it's white. I figure I'm good. White boys don' jack you for your shit—excuse the language."

"I'm walkin' into the ATM center, all enclosed, past this young dude—about twenty—who is with these two women, maybe sisters. He bumps me, bumped me when there is plenty of room around, and says, 'Excuse me!'

"I said, 'We good.'

"He says, 'I said excuse me!'

"I said, 'You excused.'

"He's following me to the ATM, and I remembered what you said about witnesses—he got them women there. What kind of fool is goin' ta throw hands under bank cameras with a policeman right around the corner? So I left, walked off saying I'll find another ATM.

"I wait for a while across the way and then go back in. Don't you know this fool—less than a third my age—comes back looking for me. I ask this man will he be my witness, tell the cops that I did not start this. He moves off, won't even look that boy's way— a grown man terrified of this young hoodlum?

"The one woman comes back and retrieves him and starts telling me how they are trying to keep him from going back to wherever they just got him out of. She was making nice but I know her and the other girl would throw me under the bus at the first sign of the law, and I would be goin' ta jail.

"So, my question to you, is what bank to use? Would Federal Hill be safe."

ATM Survival

The following is the advice I gave to Roderick, now that he has awakened in a hobbesian world where every man's hand is against him and leviathan punishes self-defense as surely as robbery.

"It's not that simple. You absolutely had to stop using the bank downtown, because there, you are perceived as the high value isolated target. Your black so the cops aren't on your side. You have money so the thugs aren't on your side. Out here you are also alone, are in the same income bracket as the locals, and—what makes you an inviting target—is you don't have any potential witnesses. A robbery on you in which you defend will just look like two knuckleheads from the city getting stupid.

"You have to go to an affluent white enclave like Federal Hill. You see, down there you're poor. The black dudes that roll into Federal Hill are looking for a softer and juicier target than you. No black man gets attacked in Federal Hill. You will not slot as prey down there. I only use the ATM machine in the neighborhood where I live in extreme circumstances. Whoever you are you are most likely to be attacked in your own neighborhood, because the attackers operating there have decided that people living there are high yield and low risk enough for them to attack."

Roderick's Parting Words

"I'm going to continue to take your advice. I'm understanding that the actual physical defense means that your survival strategy has failed and that the whole idea is to keep it non-physical until it cannot be helped.

"You know, you come up thinking that life is going to be one thing. Then you get to where you were headed all your life, and it's another. Life's a trap brother, and old age is no joke! We get old and find out they comin' for us. Ain't that the biggest lie of all."

Conclusion

What we are seeing through Roderick's eyes and often through other stories related in the Harm City vein is the deterioration of a circumscribed warrior ethic.

In the time of Roderick's grandfather black men in Baltimore had to develop a high level of combativeness to dissuade white attackers who would beat and even publicly kill lone black men for sport.

In the time of Roderick's father whites had farmed out attacking blacks to the police, and being attacked and beaten randomly by cops was just part of growing up.

By Roderick's day the cops had largely retreated to a business support role leaving the lone black youth or man at the mercy of black criminals.

Now Roderick lives in a war zone where the cops dedicate virtually all resources to combating black drug traffickers. This has cultivated a class of criminal that does not fear doing time [although they prefer not to] and use this as a lever against those like Roderick would have a deep aversion to getting locked up. The implicit threat of the street level extortionist is that the target of his threats will, if he defends himself, go to jail and/or prison and lose their ongoing source of income, emerging into the world homeless and jobless. [Most working class guys are two weeks pay from homelessness and three absences from a job loss.] The thug who gets locked up has no job based income to lose so risks less and can be bolder at the tactical level.

What has specifically placed Roderick on the urban crime menu is the reduced physicality of black youths, who are currently as combat ineffective as the cowardly whites have traditionally been, and therefore seek older and less dangerous prey.

The starkly predatory nature of personal crime comes courtesy of the geniuses that conceived of and have managed the Drug War. As the government goon squads have brought more and more ineffective pressure on the drug gangs, these gangs have evolved purely predatory second tier [not apex predation] behaviors, and, as the actual leaders of the community, have instilled this hyena-like pack ethos among the youth who come of age in their shadow; youth who are conditioned from the cradle to perceive their one and only value as a menace to less ruthless humans.

Good luck out there Roderick.

'The Cigar Cult'

Rowry Davis on Getting Busted and Harassed by the Feds

© 2014 James LaFond

This past weekend in Ohio I spoke with an old friend of mine about his experiences in a state of the Union that he did not wish to name in case any of the federal goons that have been harassing him actually read my site, which I sincerely hope they do not.

After some reflection I suppose it was all my fault, my laziness—smoking too much pot perhaps. I had a medical marijuana license, cost me three-fifty a year. I was over re-registering by about a week. The paperwork was sitting on the kitchen counter when seven body-armored guys with machineguns and two attack dogs came crashing in. My face is pressed against the floor and I'm being zip-tied while these guys are screaming commands. I have a gun against my head.

I did not even have a personal quantity of pot, just a few plants and a bunch of equipment. I had a very nice lighting array. Initially I had thought it was some kind of conspiracy—perhaps something to do with that census taker that I wouldn't talk to. But in retrospect, it was just the State bringing the hammer down on me for not paying the three-hundred-and-fifty dollar fee.

So now I can't even smoke!

They took all my stuff and piled it out in the yard next to this mobile command center—a big armored vehicle.

I said to the cop who was talking, "Why the machine guns and the dogs and the armored fighting vehicle?"

"Mister Davis we just want to go home."

"But I'm a marijuana grower?"

"Mister Davis we just want to go home to our families. You were lucky you were home or your parrot would be dead. If you had not answered the door we would have flash-banged your place."

"Let me ask you then, how many marijuana growers have fought you guys? I don't even own a gun. I'm non violent!"

"Mister Davis, there is always a first time, and we just want to go home."

Now this is when it got really bizarre. I was out in my yard on my knees, wrists zip-tied behind me, all of my stuff, thousands of dollars worth of equipment so that I could grow the highest quality cannabis possible. Now these seven goons bring my chairs outside and arrange them in a semi-circle facing away from me, and light up cigars and smoke.

What the fuck?

In the lock up they treated me with great respect, as if I were a visiting dignitary. But the black dudes, oh my God! This is a federal detention center. I have a lawyer, am set to get out by the end of the week. I'm being held with a bunch of black dudes who gave me no shit what-so-ever. I wasn't the enemy, nor was I the enemy of their enemy. I was passing through. The guards would come and get these black dudes one-by-one and beat the shit out of them. Then they would drag them off and you never see them again.

I did talk to one dude in there, a pimp with a very engaging personality. He told me to absolutely not try and get my stuff back. He said if I did succeed in getting back my things I would wake up every morning to cops parked outside my house—would not be able to use a public restroom without cops shadowing me. So all my stuff gets sold on E-bay.

Now, as I'm working on selling the place and moving away I still want to grow something, wanted a little vegetable garden outside. I'm a grower at heart, would like to have a self-sustaining farm some day. So I bought a 22 caliber rifle for pests. I don't have a felony against me, so could have bought a handgun legally—I had the right. My lawyer told me I had the right.

I pay for the firearm, and there is a waiting period. Before I head back to the gun store an Agent Vincenza of the ATF calls me up and tells me that he does not want me to have this gun. I told him that my lawyer said I have the right to this gun. He told me that he knew that but he still did not want me to have this gun. He finally said, "You know Mister Davis, I would not want to see you lose your money.

If you can bring a friend to the gun store so that I can assure that ownership is being transferred from the merchant to him rather than to you, then you can recover your payment from your friend."

My lawyer told me that this was a violation of my rights but that I should just let it go, that I couldn't fight it. So my friend and I show up at the gun store at the appointed time and these two ATF agents are there. One of them looks like a new guy on the job, stiff, just following the other guy around. The other guy introduces himself as Agent Vincenza, and guess what, he's stoned!

We do the transfer and they check my friend out and it is all so insane being that this is all happening under the supervision of a totally stoned ATF agent. This guy was nodding out, slurring his words and rolling his eyes back into his head. Look, I know high, and this dude was high!

So now I'm working odd jobs for these uneducated rural people who do not even know how to operate their own machinery. I like the West though, would like to move back out there where there is so much visual clarity when you look out on the land. I just need to find a farm somewhere and I'll be happy.

'Speaking a Different Language'

A Latino Concert Security Misadventure

© 2014 James LaFond

Back in the early 1990s Raphael and three other Puerto Rican martial artists landed a cool weekend security job providing secondary security for a heavy metal concert. These guys were not exactly heavy metal fans—I don't even know what the music they listened to back then was called, but it wasn't Holy Diver or Hell Bent for Leather.

After the show at this outdoor venue they were patrolling the grounds, having been brought on as perimeter security, not stage security or front door men. Between the equipment trucks and the back stage area they found "some stoner white boy" "drunk and high out of his mind" staggering round without a backstage pass or even a ticket.

"Well" says Raphael, "this place was crawling with drugged up poorly groomed whiteboys. We grabbed him and he struggled a little bit. You couldn't even understand what this individual was saying he was so messed up, like he was speaking a different language. He wasn't really a threat. But he was not cooperative, so we jacked him—maybe lumped him up a little—and tossed him out the back gate. Sometime later, our connection, the guy that had hired us, informed us that we had beat up Ozzy Osbourne and that we were fired! Now what kind of millionaire celebrity staggers around in the dark stoned out of his mind mumbling to inanimate objects?"

That made about as much sense as hiring skinheads to provide security for Snoop Dog.

JayZee

A Black on Black Case Study in Violent Crime

© 2014 James LaFond

JayZee is a 58 year old black female alcoholic. She is a kind soul, but receives little kindness from men, for, at a distance, she appears male. She is light skinned, and walks with a cane, which is required due to an injury resulting from a street beating and/or a drunken fall. JayZee is not homeless, but lives in such cramped squalor that she can be counted on to carry all of her worldly valuables with her. Street people are targeted for violence by thugs at a high rate for three reasons:

1. the cops and press are not sympathetic

2. there is no family to retaliate, otherwise these people would not be on the street

3. street people carry what little money they have on them, as any roommates they may have cannot be trusted

JayZee was drunk—and had hence sinned against American values and deserves what she got and will not be a candidate for liberal sympathies—on October 2nd, walking down Harford Road in a state of inebriation, she was approached by two black teens and attacked. She blacked out. The next thing she recalls is that she came to consciousness over by Chesaco Avenue about a mile away. She was still being attacked and beaten. The black adults just looked on, did and said nothing. Two unaffiliated black teens called the police on their cell phones. The police did not arrive in time to make an arrest—as far as she can remember—and the other teens stood by as witnesses but did not come to her aid.

JayZee spent the next 13 days in the hospital, until the swelling of her face was reduced enough so that she could see. Her eyes are still a mass of broken blood vessels and her cheeks are blue-black on her milk-chocolate toned skin.

Her cane was retrieved by the witnesses so she still has that to hobble around on. JayZee called the police to ask for a report on her case, as she does not even know if there was an arrest and if it is being investigated. The police officer she spoke to said that a copy of the police report would cost her $15.

JayZee won't have any money until her disability check comes out on the first of November. Some employees at the local supermarket are feeding JayZee, purchasing food for her when she comes to the store.

The 'black community' does not advocate for JayZee, does not know she exists, for she does not have a welfare mother to play to the white liberal press on her behalf, and has not been martyred in the phony war against the white police.

The white liberal media does not care about JayZee, or any marginalized person like her, because she has not been attacked by white police, who represent a bastion of political conservatism and right wing sympathy.

Not qualified to be a pawn in the phony race war that simultaneously serves to build liberal coalitions among the electorate *and* support for military style policing among the marginalized conservative opposition, JayZee will remain undefended, and un-avenged by a society who has no use for her.

Whether you, the reader, are white or black or Latino, liberal or conservative, I wager that you have already found a reason why JayZee deserves her plight. Liberals will note her alcoholism. Conservatives will take exception to a 58 year old drawing disability. The functional genius of the criminal class is that they instinctively cull the least sympathetic from among the human herd. Only when they have the audacity to attack a cow or a calf or stand up to a dominant bull will they be perceived as a menace to the herd.

10/17/14

'Yo Shorty'

A Whiff of Corporate America's Agenda

© 2014 James LaFond

I spoke with Maryann yesterday, for the first time on over a year. Maryann is not her real name of course. Rather I chose that moniker for her to pay homage to her stunning resemblance to the petite brunette actress who played Maryann in the ancient sitcom Gilligan's Island. This young lady worked for The Bank of America and had decided on going to work for a legal firm, largely due to the deteriorating nature of her working conditions for this iconic financial institution. Below is her summary of what the last month on the job was like.

Maryann

"It had just turned into a customer service job, everybody working eleven to eight manning the phones to speak with irate debtors who seem to savor the C-word as the apogee of verbal expression in English. Dealing with the credit customers once the financial side went down, that has always been bad. What I don't understand is why management decided to acquire new hires from that same level of society.

"Attire had always been professional. We wore dresses and suits, business casual at worst. Of course, when you require that level of dress you can't very well pay your people minimum wage. They dropped the dress code and replaced the downsized employees with ghetto people making eight dollars an hour.

"As it was the middle class blacks dressed like whores even with the dress code. With the dress code abolished you can only imagine what these people were wearing in the office. We had employees fist-fighting in the office. One employee defecated in the elevator—and was fired for that. Then two other employees had sex in the elevator, on the clock, doors opening and shutting, people waiting, them getting it on. These two females got into it over a guy and the one hit the other with her car on the lot—hit her, not her car, right in the hip.

"The last straw for me was going to the coffee pot, in my business casual attire, between calls during which I'm being cussed out by these nasty Tennessee rednecks, and having this eighteen year old thug come up behind me—not a stone's throw from the corporate office—wearing a hooded sweatshirt and whispering in my ear, "Yo Shorty— you cute. How 'bout yo give me yo numba?"

"Oooo yuck! If that is the kind of employee you want operating your company, then I don't want to work for you. I am very happy where I am, working for professional ladies and gentlemen who can have a conversation without the C-word, the F-bomb and the B-word which honestly seems to be beyond the ability of most adults in our current society. Really, why cuss constantly? Why is it a must?"

The 'red flag' of incivility that Maryann singled out for the focus of her distaste for banking is to me one of the surest signs of a slide in the capacity of our population to think. Most of the adults I know, even those with university degrees, are incapable of speaking a paragraph worth of dialogue without using one of the 7 formerly taboo words that have become the pillars of American expression. I think even George Carlin would be horrified. Last month I counted how many words I would have used in place of the f-words spoken to me in conversations, or overheard in close proximity, over the course of a day and it came to 23words in 71 usages.

That represents a severe restriction in vocabulary, 1 in 23, and I am not exactly Cicero.

Restricted vocabulary indicates restricted thought.

Restricted thought is indicative of a malleable mind. And, a malleable mind, what more does a tyrant need?

Is it an accident that our current tyranny of political correctness seeks to narrow permissible forms of expression, seeks to limit the number and variation of our allowed words?

If so, that does make sense.

What does not make sense is why we would concurrently limit our range of expression at the same time that the most profitable and ubiquitous businesses are personal communications outlets, like the Verizon store that I could barely squeeze into this past Saturday to get my 8 year old cell phone updated.

This pandemic of articulation suicide might just amount to the members of a society in decline emulating the lower class. But could it be something else, something more insidious?

Narco State Anatomy

The Crackpot Owner's Manual for Your Ankle-strapped Handgrips

© 2014 James LaFond

I am not a conspiracy theorist. I do, however, regard organizations as social organisms, living things that, like humans, have a conscious process, and a subconscious drive to survive, which, when successful, morphs into a drive to thrive. The individual components of a thriving organization tend to make many decisions and take many actions which result in the strengthening of that social organism. Do you, for instance, think about breathing?

Perhaps the most salient metaphor for this 'subconscious political will' is team sports, most notably football of the American variety.

The average idiot sees a company, a polity, or a military formation as a top down expression of one person's autocratic will. The entire reason for the sham presidential elections every four years is the reinforcement of this peasant mentality to see the great lord in his great house as the fount of all things good and ill. In its current form, one might actually equate the second term of a modern president to the ancient practice of assigning a scapegoat to take the blame for a community's misfortune.

To better understand the living nature of social organisms the football team makes for a nice example, for it is such an organism, if only intended as a diversion for the brutish masses so that they might not come to understand the activities of their masters for what they are. The football team further makes an ideal example for a thriving and striving social organism because its workings are grossly apparent. Where much of the running of a baseball team is done by obscured men crouching gnome like in their dens, the football coaching staff is almost entirely visible, as are the support staff and the various squads of players at rest and play, all visible simultaneously.

Any look at a football team—on the field and on the sideline—will reveal a complex multifaceted social organism focused on a number of very obvious tasks. The game will reveal the head coach as merely one of perhaps a hundred moving parts in a machine whose every gear seems to have the opportunity for–at least temporarily—autonomous action. And, like the law of unintended consequences cited by libertarian thinkers when discussing social engineering, one can never predict the exact outcome of a football play.

Keeping in mind the inertia and unpredictable consequences of the actions of social organisms, let's enumerate the basic equation whereby the illicit drug economy has become the social driver in the postmodern world.

1. Rich politicians take working class and middle class money to pay poor women to avoid marriage and spawn armies of feral youths, thereby guaranteeing cultural decay, rendering the population ripe for stage 3.

2. That welfare money gushes up the economic latter to superrich corporations by many and diverse ways; traveling from middle, to poor, to rich like a boomerang of inequity.

3. The purposeless poor, idle rich, despondent working class, and shrinking middle class turn to

drugs to deaden the pain of this inauthentic existence. As I write most Americans are either legally or illegally medicated against pain, stress, depression, anxiety, or—my favorite—addiction!

4. The rich politicians criminalize drugs, accelerating the suction of money from the ghetto to the penthouse and simultaneously the growth of the state at the expense of the middle class and working class.

5. The resulting Narco State, built on the sham drug war and the booming drug trade, wages continuous external war and warns of a coming internal war against terrorists.

6. The Narco State is, by means I do not fully understand, here, apparently to stay, and so long as it fails to win the drug war that it wages, will continue to thrive.

7. Just as victory in the internal drug war would emasculate the Narco State, victory over, or peace with, the external Islamist forces could expose the drug war for the sham it is—so the Manhattan versus Mecca proxy war most not be fought to a conclusion or abandoned.

Narco State Nuance

Law Enforcement in a Puritanical/Hedonistic Society

© 2014 James LaFond

Suburban motorists seem to understand the State Police. They understand that at certain times, quarterly in some states, that troopers are rated on how much revenue they have brought in writing speeding tickets. This middle-class cop incentive is easy to grasp.

What about the working class cop down in the ghetto?

Due to the shrinking municipal tax base mid-sized cities like Baltimore can only field a police force with federal subsidies—kind of like a small militarized Middle Eastern country with no oil revenue needing U.S. subsidies to keep its troops in the field. With the subsidized money come stipulations from the federal government, generally tied to two things: fighting the Drug War, and fighting terrorism, both of which require law enforcement and militarized police using population sweep tactics to supplant traditional community-based policing.

Policing, as the American mind has traditionally conceived it; of having a local sheriff, or a beat cop, does not exist in mid-sized American cities, as policing is not compatible with fighting a global insurgency or with enforcing puritanical laws on a godless population.

Policing, in mid-sized cities has given way to law enforcement, making 'protect and serve' mottos anachronistic at best.

I am no friend of the police, but have interviewed a few, and have paid attention to their plight. [Note: for a pro police view from another fringe writer see Fred Reed's website fredoneverything, for which there is a link on our network page.] However, I understand that most of what cops do that I disagree with is precisely what they have been tasked to do. As a Darwinist I don't expect any man to jeopardize his job standing up for something as fleeting as morality.

Urban police, like suburban and rural state troopers, are expected to log a certain number of actions, determined by department policy and priorities and also in response to political and media pressure. In Baltimore for example, If Eyewitness News' 'Eye Team' reporters go on air citing proof that the last 10 homicides attributed to drug dealing in West Baltimore have gone unsolved, and charges are made that it is because these victims are black—when in reality it is because they are drug dealers and no witnesses will talk for fear of retaliation—police will be pulled from traditional business support and preventive duty to round up corner boys who will just be released by the court commissioner on Monday, temporarily leaving certain business districts un-policed.

Overall the greatest distorting effect of the War on Terror is the federal government's demand for proof of enforcement in the form of documented traffic stops of suspicious motorists near, for example, Martin's Air Force Base, even though 24 of these stops are of Mary of the goddess like figure who slices ham at the deli across the street by the same three all-too-human cops.

In the city the feds demand arrests of the criminal population, with, in one particular year a decade ago, the Harm City police actually arresting 1 in 5 residents, including almost every boxer in town! Of course this is grossly in efficient, but there are logical reasons. Let me give you one example from one cop who was nice enough to discuss his dilemma with me.

Bill—not his real name—is a Northeastern District cop, who agreed to speak with me about why he was pulling me up, a 50 year old pedestrian, while he ignored the three groups of youths who were even then prowling the neighborhood looking for mugging victims.

"Okay Sir, if you were copping dope, you are in steady commission of a crime from that house back down there on Echodale I saw you leave, up until this point where I pull you over—all the way to your own front door, and beyond, into this residence and that residence.

"On the other hand, those hoodrats who you claim are out looking for mugging victims—and I believe you Sir—they are not committing a crime until they lay a hand on someone and they will never do that while I'm cruising by. Besides, based on what you are describing, they are working together, using their mommies' smart phones to triangulate my position. How am I going to police that by myself, out here on my own Sir?

"Additionally, most locals on foot like you will not report being mugged to me, because they have a history with us, and have that animosity. It's a lose-lose situation Sir."

At this point 'Bill' got a call for a 'domestic disturbance' as he characterized it, and was off, reinforcing the fixed point and line-of-sight nature of car-mobile urban policing. He is an officer who is expected to produce, and production in the Drug War is much more doable than proof of protecting and serving common citizens in need. Just like athletes always adapt their methods and habits to the rules of the sport as they morph along the line of societal expectation, so does the law officer adapt his behavior to the changing rules dictated by his masters, who grow increasingly distant from his arena of action.

I, from my vantage among the population that Bill is tasked with 'policing', see no way in which his organization can effectively police in the traditional manner while doing Drug War law enforcement according to federal guidelines, and under the counterproductive pressures often brought by politics and the media.

For the common occupant of a Narco State town like Baltimore I recommend developing habits that will keep you off Bill's to-do list while simultaneously using awareness and avoidance methods for surviving the smart phone using youths we discussed, who are members of a protected, privileged and state-subsidized class who may not be addressed by him according to his rules of engagement until after they hit you or me.

The Narco State is in my view a type of earthly purgatory designed by a committee of old fashioned leftist liberals and new fangled puritan neo-conservatives; people at odds with both the conservative nature of their law officers and the nihilistic nature of their urban slaves.

The police officer or law officer, such as he is, is as powerless as you and I, and has less impact on this environment than the violent criminals he is alternately sent after and barred from interfering with by his masters.

The Narco State must and will fall. Until then I'm enjoying reporting on the dystopian mess.

American Woman

Gonna Get You Killed

© 2014 James LaFond

Yesterday I had a date with a nice lady. This was the kind of date that was once common in ages past, and becomes increasingly more common as one ages. Megan and I met at her house so that I could walk her to the corner store a half mile off, so that she might enjoy the walk and not have to run the gauntlet of teen age boys who normally challenge this 50-something woman to fist fight, or threaten rape openly on the street, or simply call her a 'white bitch' as they flex, pose, and grab their genitals in chimpanzee conquest rituals.

Megan is a 'liberated' 'semi-feminist' child of the 70s who believes that men and women are mentally and morally equal but that males are so physically superior it is ridiculous for a woman to expect to be able to defend herself, and she must thereby seek the protection of a man.

Narco Night Train

As we walked by white alcoholics arguing on the street, black youths skulking on street corners and in alley mouths eyeing me with smoldering reticence for denying them their prey, and no less than three huge houses—former mansions—that have been converted to half way houses for the derelict white drug addicts and sex offenders crowding the wrap around porches, she was able to enjoy the autumn breeze, even as the autumn of the civil world she was born into gives way to a predatory winter.

As she reveled in her freedom via escort I chaffed, becoming increasingly prone to a violent outburst should we be approached. Here was the rub that is even now still bothering me.

Megan is a modern Western Woman who does not believe in walking behind a man. Her impulse—certainly enhanced by my full set of teeth and lack of body odor—to want to walk beside me, was as much caused by her desire to enjoy a conversation as it was by her feminist indoctrination, but was at odds with my purpose, protecting her.

We may think that men walking ahead of women in 'less civilized nations' is an act of diminishment, a means of dehumanizing the woman. Only a decadent culture of extreme plenty and cozy coup blinders could think this.

The entire time I walked with Megan and she sought to walk by my side I continually worried about her being in harm's way either from traffic on the right, or an alley or doorway assault from the left, in which she could be used as a hostage against me. What was even worse was her obstruction of one hand or the other. If she is on my right her impulse to get close if we are assaulted could impede my weapon draw. If she is on my left she is only good for a human shield and I am supposed to be her shield.

By the time we got to the store I was so irritated over this that I was either going to scold her, which would have ruined her day, and my chances at that plate of lasagna that had brought me hither, or act out aggressively toward any approaching males. If the woman is not cooperating with me during a walk by staying behind and in line with me within two paces, then I opt for preemptive strikes against any suspicious males, which is legally perilous.

Fortunately no one stepped up to me so her walk was as joyful as she had hoped. If this would have been in a worse area or at night, I would have stopped and insisted she walk behind right off the bat. This episode points out the dilemma of walking in a predatory world with the curiously counterintuitive creature that is Western Woman accompanying you in her domestic state of bliss engendered by her status as a woman of the greatest empire the world has ever known, as she walks witlessly down into the criminal wasteland blooming from its rotting heart.

Before I'm dead I will not be surprised if I have occasion to scold a female companion in ancient Robert E. Howard fashion as I walk through the ruins of this once great medieval city, "Wench, if you grab my sword arm again you shall know the back of my hand! Now behind me and be mindful of the shadows."

Be a man. It is all the more enjoyable for being a sin.

Stoners in the Basement

Aldo, on Being a Home Owner in the Narco State

© 2014 James LaFond

Yesterday, after I walked Megan back to her place, and declined the plate of lasagna that had bought me hither because her roommate's cigarette smoking ruined my appetite, I journeyed home through some of the lesser alleys and side streets of Northeast Baltimore.

On a grass-paved side street—I kid you not—I walked by a yard in which a 120 pound pitbull hurled itself at me against its master's fence, chomping and salivating for my blood like my fictional animalistic action hero Jay Bracken wanting to eat a homosexual future cop alive. I noted the quality of the ragged slurp of flexing jaws for my next Jay-bone scene, and wondered if there was anything I could do to keep this thing from eating me with only a razor blade in my pocket.

Heading down a heavily shaded adjoining side street I walked by a man and his two boys playing ball, an act that whites no longer engage in as they vegetate at their videogame console.

I came to the main drag and—still irritably aggressive over my walk with the woman who wanted my protection but insisted on walking next to me—stepped out onto the center line to let the traffic go both ways. A young fellow with braids, smoking a blunt in a '98 Toyota, stopped and waved for me to cross. I gave him a wave and jogged across and through an alley to another side street.

As I emerged from the alley I ran into Aldo and Evers, two Northeast Baltimore characters. Here is what I can recall of Aldo's end of our conversation:

"Hey Jimmy, this is Evers. Evers, Jimmy, former Master of Hell. I used to work for him—ruthless dude. Ruthless but fair.

"You gained weight Jimmy—like twenty pounds. Evers, mutherfucker used to fight. Now he writes stories. He ought to beat the shit out of Sol.

"You know Sol got married three months back to that poor girl—don't know what the hell she was thinking. He's living in a doorway or something with his dog now, who seems to be the big loser in the divorce. Anyways, you know I have Herman living in the basement—he's recovering from that shoulder operation and can't work so he's got a free home. I take care of my people. The other day—last week—Sol comes over while I'm gone and sneaks downstairs, wakes Herman up and beats the shit out of him with his guitar, trying to get him to leave so he can have the apartment.

"Dillon was home so she told Sol—lied because you know I hate the pigs and don't want them in my house—and told him she had called the cops and he skedaddled before Herman got hurt too bad. I just got some of my intestine removed—thought it was a regular hernia but was worse, so I'm not kicking his ass. I talked to Sol down on the corner. Now he respects me. What does he say, he uses the opportunity to try and talk me into putting Herman out and letting him live down there. I suppose jaggermister does that to the brain.

"Well, I suggested he fight you for your apartment—being as he got put out so you could have a place to write. But he was like, "Naw, Jimmy will beat the shit out of me all week long—fucker is evil and don't get tired.'

"So here is what I said, 'You know, you should ask Jimmy for a stick fighting lesson, and maybe he will find you a place to live.' I said that hoping you would beat his ass.

"Oh, that's right, it's an honorable pursuit and you don't do that. That's too bad. Thought the plan was kind of diabolic myself."

This is how our conversation ended.

"Well Aldo, the boys are coming back out to scrimmage on Saturday. We've taken the month off. And Cory, he has dibs on fresh meat. I'd be honor bound to train and corner Sol to my best ability. But if he agrees to roll with Cory…"

Aldo's Dracula like continence lightened to a brighter pallor of gloom and he grinned wolfishly at Evers as Evers [a tiny toothless copper-skinned black man] cackled with hand-rubbing glee, and Aldo intoned hollowly, "Cory, the giant Viking dude! Good night! Herman will like that! Take care Jimmy.'

And we were off on our separate ways, up one alley and down another.

Running From the Cops

What can I say, I'm a fan of the sport.

Running From The Cops #1

A Public Service Guide for the Spry Ghettoite

© 2012 James LaFond

"Fat Cop, Fat Cop, what you gonna do when I run from you!"

-Hamad "Too Quick fo da Thick" Jones

I have done many things in my life.

Running from the police is not one of them.

I have seriously considered doing almost everything that I have not actually done, including dating Prime Minister Thatcher.

I have never seriously considered running from the cops.

For this reason, I have begun accessing my database of those elite few, who have run from the cops. These fellows are hard to pin down for interviews, and–as their 'flight from might' propensities are not always appreciated by The Man—they are often housed in places that would make it inconvenient for me to conduct an interview. I'm sorry Hamad, but as compelling as your saga surely is, I am not going to submit to a body cavity search, just so I can get the whole story.

Just as with any athletic undertaking, you need to approach running from the cops as a science or an art. Let's set the stage.

The Blue Team

In your interest, I have done my best to interview the opposition, the guys with the cars, guns, radios, dogs, helicopters and jails. All I can say is that I tried son.

"Oh, don't even make me get up outta dis cruiser en chase ya boy. You will be sorry—money back guarantee!"

-Officer Searles, 2002

"Really, I talk to them from the cruiser—yell down the alley while my younger partner earns his shield chasing their young asses. I use the car as much as possible. But that is only really practical when you are working with another officer. We don't see the chopper much on the Southside. Probably the fact that it is a peninsula with limited egress is our greatest advantage down here. And with the urban homesteading—all the yuppies in their nice flats— there are not a lot of vacants for the trash to duck into—none really. I'd say we bag them more often than not."

-Anonymous Officer, from 2001

Okay, you heard the man, run into a crappy neighborhood—your neighborhood, not some white bread real estate commercial.

Coach Nate

Now that we have heard from the opposition, just as with any sport, you need a coach; an old hand; long retired from the game; who has seen it all. Let's see what he has to say. This past July, as I headed through the Inner Harbor to train, I ran into a famous old school 'hoodlum', retired of course. He is about 60, 'but used ta run from some Five 'O back in da day now.'

"Okay, you mus not have any kine a weapon or whatnot—den yo ass jus' shot. If not da Helicopter will be on yo ass fo sure.

"Do not talk to the police; that when the otha be circlin'. If dey stopped yo ass dey already called backup!

"Do not have no history of fightin' no cop—cause when dey catch ya dat shit will be bad. In fact, if you even look dangerous—a big black man—do not run. I told you now. Get yo big ass on the pavement; 'yessir, yesssir, again sir', en so on. When a police is chasin' ya he cannot be scared. You want him to enjoy that shit, get evigorated. If he falls en get hurt or somethin', you bes' not ged caught.

"Now, situations where it make sense ta run is genally limited to kids. Unless you shootin' people, most adults just should not run. Kids get in much less trouble with the court for runnin' 'cause dey kine a expected ta run.

"So, lez sayin' you with your friends when shit goes down, which usually is the way, the bes' thing you can hope for is that you got a loudmouth dumbass friend that will tussle wit da police en give you the clean getaway. The cops much prefer beatin' da shit outta some dumbass den chasin' some fast hopper. A course, if yo cain't run, jus' sit yo ass on the curb."

Slam

Slam is an infamous skinhead who has quite a history. Let him clue you in on some of the finer points brought into play by coach Nate's line of reasoning. Think of Slam as the Defensive Coordinator.

"I've been in a few gangs. The first one was when I was in Korea. We army brat kids hada gang that fought the Korean kids. You definitely did not want to get caught by MPs or Korean cops. By the time I was living back here I had it down to a science. I have never been caught by the cops.

"Number one is to always wear two different shirts when you go out to commit a crime, and a hat. After everyone runs you toss the hat and one of the shirts.

"Number two is you do not run but walk. Your stupid friends are running, let them draw the heat. It is the reason why you have friends to begin with, so you can get away with your crime. And, let's face it; most criminals are pretty stupid, particularly young ones.

"Last, but not least, is you walk toward the sirens. The cops will just blow by you. A school book is a nice touch if you can swing it. You just have to stay cool brother."

Caley

Caley was a young drug dealer in Dundalk, in Southeastern Baltimore County. He did not do well running from the cops himself, and has referred me to his cousin Steevo, who had such a history of running from the cops that he will get his own article. Before I prepare to interrogate Steevo, let's end with a cautionary note from his oft caught cousin.

"Don't run from them fat Dundalk cops. That shit ain't gonna happen. That's a hazard to your health. When they catch you they'll beat you with a phone book so it won't leave marks. Fat cops fuck you up. Sayin' a fat cop can't run is like sayin' a fat chick ain't athletic. Take a turkey leg from her and she will chase you, and catch you, and shove it up your ass. You really need to talk to Steevo; he's one of them crazy ones that don't care about pissing off the cops. Me, I like my bacon with my eggs and that's it. You won't catch me runnin'."

Running From The Cops #2

Steevo Shakin' & Bakin' on The City Line

© 2013 James LaFond

I recently sought out and interviewed a famous teenage hood-rat from the far Eastside of town; the neighborhood of Saint Helena in Dundalk Maryland, about two hundred yards from the Baltimore City line. Steevo is a stocky, tattooed fellow with a mild-mannered disposition, sporting painful-looking art on his neck. The last time I ran into him I let him know that his interrogation was imminent. So, when he saw me walking toward him the other night with a pen and pad he grinned widely, "So what's up dude?"

"For how long were you a hoodlum?"

"I stopped getting in trouble by seventeen or eighteen, though I was still doing stupid shit like selling weed when I was twenty-one. Shit started up when I was thirteen; selling weed in bars by the time I was fourteen.

"Why did you stop?"

"I realized that I could go to Big Boy Jail, that it wouldn't just be calling Mom to pick your ass up from the precinct anymore."

"I heard you ran from the cops on occasion."

"Hell yeah! Us little bastards ran from the cops all the time. We would even do it to fuck with them. You see a cop, and you all just split up and run like you did something and they have to chase you. Of course we would get in trouble too. We'd start some shit in the County and then hop over the line into the City and act like we didn't do shit."

"For the up and coming hoodlums out there, do you have any general advice on running from the cops?"

"They're faster than you think! Had me fooled a couple of times! Just run and pray to God they give up. We didn't hide or nothin'. We knew the ins and outs of the entire neighborhood; knew where we were goin' to run before we turned the corner; knew what was around the corner. One-way streets are important. There were some one-way streets where people double parked and the cops wouldn't even bother driving down there. There was this one spot we called the Grass Alley. We'd make them chase us down there because they had to get out and run. Of course then you have a pissed off cop!

"Sometimes we would get tired of runin' and just go sit in the McDonalds and let it blow over. Not once did they ever check in the McDonalds. I guess they thought we were just stupid kids.

"All of that shit is a lot harder to get away with now. I wish it was as easy as it was back then. The money came in so quick it was ridiculous. Never once did any of us get busted on the drug shit. We just got caught up in stupid shit, just running to fuck with the cops; bullshit stuff. The business end was easy...thirteen, fourteen years-old sitting in the bar getting drunk and selling weed. We didn't really have to worry about getting caught doing it in bars with a bar on every block on back streets.

"And you would get a heads up. We had this one dude on Baltimore Avenue who's dad was friends with a cop. One day we're sittin' in 'is yard on lawn chairs smokin' weed and this fuckin' cop pulls up and walks up into the yard, and I about shit. We're hiding our shit and the dad's kid says, 'What the fuck are you doin'?'

"I said, 'Dude, did you not just see that fuckin' cop walkin' up in your old man's fuckin' yard?'

"He's like, 'Its cool, he's friends with my old man.'

"So it was like that. The cop would come out to where we sold the shit and tell us which houses were goin' to get busted, and when the raid was comin'.

"Well that's one way not to have to run. You basically stay out of trouble by knowing when shit is coming down and not being there. You could say that a lot of the runin' was for spite, and to fuck with certain cops, like Officer Horse—what a dick he was!"

Steevo and I were interrupted in our sublime quest to define the Hood-rat Holy Grail. He did promise that the next time we meet the true tale of dealing with, and running from, Officer Horse, legendary bane of Dundalk street kids, will be told.

Running From The Cops #3

Steevo on Officer Horse

© 2013 James LaFond

What, a, dick! Officer Horse was a complete douche-bag—a pig. He's the kind of cop who's a cop with or without the badge. We never saw him off duty, but he had that 'better than everybody else' attitude.

I was thirteen. We hung in Saint Helena and Old Dundalk, always between three and six of us. We sold drugs but mostly in bars or at prearranged times. It's not like we carried the shit around with us. I mean we were kids but we weren't stupid! Every time he saw you he would stop you, get out of the car, give you shit—just being a dick. 'You boys causin' trouble?'

He would make us empty our pockets—turn them inside out, so that everything hit the ground; money, cigarettes—that's it. My buddy Mat said, 'It's none of your fuckin' business!' he pulled him

up, threw him in the car and took him home to his
mom. She was cool with it—used to buy us beer
and whatever. My mom would flip though, so I
always said I lived with Mat.

We'd see him comin' down the street—knew the
number of his car. We all just took off in different
directions, just to fuck with him because he fucked
with us. He's a cop so he's got to chase you right? I
ran from him maybe ten-twelve times and only got
caught twice. He would catch Little Ryan all the
time. Ryan was a little shit—like eight—and he
wanted to hang with us, so he was like our chaff,
our cop countermeasure.

The two times he caught me were basically
identical—I'm a chunky cigarette smoking kid and
he's a full-on man. I was quick out of the gate, but if
he locked in on you and you were a smoker, good
night, unless you hit the Grass Alley. If we hit the
Grass Alley we usually lost him. He would kick your
heels out from underneath of you—bam, slam,
hittin' the fucking concrete face first! That part
definitely sucked man. Fat boy took a roll—felt like
shit! He didn't need no knee in the back or any of
that shit. He's a big manly man and I'm a fat little
kid. He would cuff you while you are on your face,
then yank you up by your arms. Now that shit hurt.

Once we were drinkin' in the yard next door to Mat's house and he rolls up, asking us what we are doing, 'Where are your parents at!'

Mat said, 'Fuck you pig! Ain't none of your business!'

Horse said, 'So you're going to be a little smartass huh?' and grabbed his ass up!

He grabbed him, cuffed him, and went to take him to his car, which was pretty stupid 'cause his house was just next door! And the pig fuckin' knew it because he had taken Mat there I don't know how many times. Of course Mat points out that he is a dumbass, 'Asshole, I live next door!' and Officer Horse slams his face into the door frame—a little high, did not break the nose, just cut his forehead. He made us leave and rode him around the block— so you're thinking is he a big faggot or what? Nothin' happened to Mat, just the embarrassment of having to sit in the cruiser in front of his house. He was already planning his revenge though—you can bet on that shit.

A couple of days later we were at the bar. I forget the name of the bar. His brother lived over top of it and it was a drug bar—cocaine I think. The cops came to raid the bar, two cop cars. Now we are on the roof, up there drinking, and there is an eve overhanging about two feet. So the cops, they pull up close, driver's side to the bar door and get out, leaving their car doors open—douche-bags! Mat sets his beer down and says, 'You want to see something funny? Watch this shit.'

So we go over to the edge of the roof above the gutter and he whips his dick out and begins pissing. It's not like he had to be a great shot or anything. Besides when you're a kid you practice pissing on stuff. He pisses right on the driver's seat dude— drains the vein! You could hear it raining on the seat. Unfortunately it was not Officer Horse's seat, but some other cops. Oh well, fuck him! We did not stick around to see him sit in it, just scooted back into his bro's apartment through the window.

Now I always watched out for the fat cops. There were a couple of these big fat boys. They had some legs that surprised you, and compared to kids who smoked they had good lungs. I saw this one big boy cop hopping a six foot fence going after one of my buddies. But still, if you scatter, they never got many.

Officer Horse was probably in his mid twenties, so I suppose is in his forties now. It's hard to recall things like their voice from when you were a kid because he just sounded like a man. He was a big ass man and you were a kid. Adults just all spoke this jerk-off 'background' [monotone] language that you tried not to hear let alone remember. Out of all the cops he was the biggest dick, the one whose name we remembered. The other cops might pull you up for smokin'. But Officer Horse, he broke your cigarettes, and then ground them into the pavement with his heels so there was nothing to salvage.

Go ahead and use his name—fuck him!

Steevo is gainfully employed, has an awesome movie collection, a good old lady, and only smokes on special occasions.

Harm City Hit & Run

Just Trying to Get a Beer in Baltimore

© 2014 James LaFond

5:15 p.m.

An hour ago I headed down to the liquor store—the Korean one, not the Punjabi one, thank you very much. John, the owner, extended me the common courtesy of rounding down the taxes on the cheapest six-pack in his cooler. As I bore my questionable brew home Big Rich called me from East Baltimore, about his time in West Baltimore on the day crew at Stop, Shop & Run.

I stopped in at the hipster bar for one beer as Big Rich regaled me with the tale of…

Tide Yo!

A fine young man, his pants hanging below his knees just so, his hat cocked just so, seemed to have lost his way. The police officer on duty at this fine urban foods emporium noticed that the man had mistaken the front door for the register lane and walked over to render aid, customer service on his mind. The customer frantically kept trying to haul his two, two-gallon jugs of tide laundry detergent out of the cart, and kept being dragged back in, 'barely a buck-ten his self'.

Miraculously our hero yanked the [$50 retail, $20 resale] haul out of the cart, and made off, the cop hot on his heels, reaching for his tazer. Our hero made it to the head of the parking lot as the cop drew a bead on him. The stairs down to the parkway were concrete, and the cop did not want a dead shoplifter on his hands. He yelled for the customer to drop the jugs and he could go. He did so. Officer Thrifty brought the haul back to the store and then alerted cops and security stationed at nearby stores.

Within an hour, our hero, Tide Yo, fell for the bait and was collared by security at Bull's Eye Big Buys and hauled off to Central Booking.

One of the new White Vice Lords—tattooed teardrops and all—came into the bar selling women's deodorant and body wash he had just stolen from the drug store two blocks away. The going price was two dollars per unit. He seemed to be fully inked except for portions of his face.

Good Evening Sir

5:40 p.m.

I walked through the grassy courtyard of the church and the rectory where four young men smoked pot and drank malt liquor. The eldest said, "Good evening Sir" and I returned the courtesy.

As I came to the main drag a group of four younger teens were joking on my side of the street so I crossed. As I did so a 'thunk' 'clunk' 'ping' and 'moan' of metal and fiber glass sounded behind me.

A youth behind the wheel of an SUV with tinted windows had side-swiped a mail truck—one of those that look like a converted German WWII staff car—on the driver's side and dragged it out into the middle of the road. The four boys were cheering him on as he struggled to get it in gear.

I was now halfway cross a side street as he tore loose a piece of fiberglass fender from his driver's side, put it in reverse, whipped it around, and gunned it up the street. He then got stuck in traffic behind the cars at the next light and his engine died. He turned it over a few times, shifted, pulled his moaning door tight, and then got it started. He banked right so I leaped onto the sidewalk in time to avoid becoming the punch line.

He did about fifty going up the side street as the sounds of sirens began to converge from two fire stations. I saw an ambulance, a pumper, and a hook and ladder. The mail truck was not moving. The police chopper was headed out to the West Side.

Hopefully the postal employee is okay.

The Jack-boot Brigade

The most noticeable effect the drug war has had on the lives of everyday people has been increased police scrutiny of suspicious behavior ranging from sitting on municipal benches and walking from one residence to another to looking a little too confident. I do what I can to cover it short of becoming the story.

Wood Shampoo Wannabes

When the Policeman is not Your Friend

© 2012 James LaFond

A Really Touchy Subject

I think this is the place where I'm supposed to remind everyone how much the police have supported me when I worked in management and security and that I even have a friend that is a police officer...

I can vouch for the special brand of fear engendered by police corruption.

My boss was followed and threatened by a group of Baltimore City cops for not permitting one of them to cash a third-party check.

As a store manager I had two cops threaten me for not opening up for them after hours.

I had a cop stalk me for over an hour once. See When You're Food.

And, most frightening of all, was when I found myself investigating a theft at work, that led directly to the off duty police officer that was supposed to handle this stuff on my behalf. I buried that, thank you very much.

I have never been afraid of the many criminals who threatened my life. Indeed, this always gave me a sense of empowerment. [Is it okay with you liberals if I borrow that buzz word? I promise to give it back. I don't want to keep it.] However, the cops who have threatened my freedom planted some un-definable dread in my gut. I can only imagine how much more frightening that would be if I were engaged in a criminal enterprise. Or, perhaps if you are a career criminal it is less threatening. I won't ever be able to tell you from firsthand experience, but maybe one day I'll take a survey of the criminals among us.

I would like to write briefly of two things that happened decades ago but that have haunted me since. And I do believe Harm City is just the place to vent this small antechamber of my psyche.

Officer Friendly

I was working overnight in a supermarket with a really nice, hardworking twenty-year-old man named Kurt. This was in the late 1980s and I was about thirty, the right age for a mentor. Kurt was very attached to his father who was dying of heart disease. It had fallen on him to support his mother and he was looking to make a living for himself. I offered to train him to take over my department manager job as I had plans on leaving the company.

One night, as we were pulling out our freight, I could tell that Kurt was troubled. I said, "What's up man—you're dad okay?"

He said, "As good as you can expect."

He then worked like a ghost for a few hours. Finally, while I was opening a valve in the base of the frozen food bunker that we had just defrosted, he placed both hands on the case rim, stared vacantly at the wall above us, and said, "I was taking a shortcut tonight [this was a Sunday night], walking up the alley behind the hardware store. The backdoor was open and this cop was loading tools in the trunk of his cruiser."

Kurt swallowed hard and looked at me, "I've never been so scared. The way the cop looked at me. He was old enough to be my dad. I hope he doesn't get caught or else he might come for me—I'm not saying a thing."

I failed that portion of my mentor exam and mumbled something about not taking the shortcut anymore.

A month later Kurt informed me that he was quitting because he had been accepted into the Baltimore City Police Academy. I responded, "Why would you want a thankless job like that? I mean this sucks, but at least we don't get sued for doing our job!"

He looked at me and grinned, "So I can get paid for beating the shit out of black guys."

Wow.

Barbara the Barbarian

Twelve years later, on one hot summer day, I was training a young female boxer at the Dundalk Senior High track in Southeastern Baltimore County. At the time I had longhair and just looked like the kind of guy cops trained to arrest. Right behind the other side of the school the Baltimore County Police had a training program. We finished our laps as these two-dozen clean-cut Ward Cleaver clones filed onto the field.

We passed them on our way to the mushroom shaped asphalt section [I think it's the shot-puting area] to do our mitt-drills. Now Barbara was a savage little thing with quite a nice butt, so there were a few cat-calls, and some mentions that if she needed a 'real man' they would take care of her. Their stoic master, who looked like he should have been a Marine Corp Drill Instructor, ignored the impropriety and then lined them up for their drills.

As Barbara hit the mitts she snarled, "You ought to call out the biggest one and beat his ass. That man in charge will let it happen. He's an animal too."

I responded coolly, "I don't like to antagonize cops. They have long memories and lots of friends."

She growled as she dug a shovel hook and my elbows lit up with pain, "I could knock 'em all out—bunch of fuckin' Boy Scouts."

I coached her on dropping her guard and she taunted me, "I'll go say something. The head guy wants me—I can get you a fair fight with one of those dickheads."

I said, "Nah, nah"—and then she dug an uppercut into my solar plexus and stepped around and planted a right hook in my kidney with a savage growl, "Just like that, bang the body..."

Now, coaching 'The Barbarian' with the mitts called for a good clinch game when she got fired up. So I clinched with her and said, "Let's go to the Rec. Center."

She said, "Okay", and I ducked the left hook that she winged at my temple before I grabbed her wrists and yanked off the bag gloves.

Barbara and I then began walking off the field as the Drill Instructor led the group in jumping-jacks and she groused, "Fucking needle-dick pigs—we should kick their asses."

Just then I noticed a set of car keys in the beaten down grass these men had just walked across to get to their present sweating position. I snatched up the keys and Barbara chirped, "Oh, we're takin' that bitch!"

I stood for a moment, looking down into her maniacal eyes and at her heaving B-cups and momentarily, within the confines of my fertile mind, lived a day in the life of Barbara The Barbarian's man-toy, beating up police cadets, taking their car to Tyrone's chop-shop on Asquith— and eating a pro-class kidney punch every time I disagreed with her...

...I emerged from my Puerto Rican Psycho-bitch escort reverie, and decided to do the right thing.

She stood there angrily with sharp-knuckled fists on her little hips as I marched over to the Drill Instructor. The men stopped drilling as he glared at them. A couple of them mumbled 'hippie' jokes and one said something about being 'pussy-whipped'.

Finally, my skinny longhaired self stood before the man who looked like he could take a beachhead, and I extended the keys, "Here sir, I think these belong to one of your men."

He looked into my eyes and said, "Thank you sir, much obliged."

I walked away from the sound of two-dozen wimps training to fight the war on drugs, hoping only that I would survive the walk to the parking lot with the pit-bull of a woman who was now glaring at me like I had worn a dress to her blood & guts workout...

Please remember to say 'sir' [and putting a yes in front of it does help]. It has saved me from the baton thus far.

Soap-on-a-Rope Stocks Projected to Soar

Notes on Our Expanding Police State

© 2013 James LaFond

Three days ago I was finishing John Perkins's, Confessions of an Economic Hit Man, reviewed in the article below. I was so enthralled with it I did not wish to get home to the estate, where the sniveling peasants might beseech me for counsel and otherwise occupy my day with their trivial concerns. Once home I write. When I walk, wait for the bus, and commute on the bus, I read. I find this to be a good inexpensive use of my time. Reading though attracts the goons. It does not attract criminals. Criminals avoid anyone insane enough to walk around reading, especially when they are dressed in a lowly laborer's work clothes.

At work three weeks ago a cop who had harassed me two years ago [See Officer ManFriendly on the Harm City page] was shopping where I work. He passed me about four times, eying me critically as he discussed shooting techniques with his partner.

211

He kept doing a double-take as I worked and he shopped on our time and our dime. By the time he was checking out I was on my break reading Voodoo Fire in Haiti on the bench by the express lane. He was turning his head and making hard eye-contact; perhaps wondering if I was indeed the 'criminal' he had harassed for the crime of walking to work one rainy night in late 2011. I had given him a website card, and he did keep doing double-takes at the book—but who knows. It just made me feel uncomfortable that he was so focused on me, an old stock clerk on the job. A young coworker came up to me and snorted a laugh as the cops left, "And those pigs wonder why we hate them!"

So, weeks later, and only a few days ago, I wended my way through the ghetto, taking the long way home in order to finish reading that great book. I have become good at reading and notating as I walk. Also, the busses are much safer than they used to be thanks to all of the smart-phone addiction. Punks now watch porn and rap videos instead of picking fights with and shaking down old grunts. As I am a fulltime writer now the book and pen are now my ever-present arsenal, the shield and sword with which I must defend myself if attacked.

Apparently cops know this, that books; even Mister Perkin's cheap flimsy best-seller, are deadly weapons. For, as I walked along a city lane reading and taking notes, I was shadowed by a city cop who crept along observing me, stopping when I stopped, from the comfort of her environmentally controlled Chariot of God-as-government. I eventually sat and looked at her. Then I began taking down her cruiser number and license plate and she pulled off.

I do not know if I will be so bold in the future after reading these two recent postings on RT.com:

1. 6/6/13 05:53, The New York State Senate has passed a law that makes it a felony to backtalk a cop. Thanks for giving them the excuse you 'Occupy' twerps.

2. 6/7/13 01:44, the US Department of Justice just completed a survey of one third of the nation's juvenile detention facilities, in which they interviewed 8,500 inmates, 1,720 of which claimed to have been raped. One out of five of these teens claimed to have been raped more than ten times, predominantly by staff. The majority of the abuse claims were made in Ohio, Illinois, South Carolina and Georgia. Do I really want to get locked up with the predators that graduate from these facilities

into the Big House just to assert my right to free speech in the face of petty tyranny?

These seem just like little cracks in the fabric of the mass delusion called Freedom. But coupled with the increased boldness of cops willing to nose into my crime-free middle-aged literary life, the massive monitoring of our electronic communications by the Federales, and snail mail letters from two readers who have told me that they cannot purchase my e-books and must view the site through other people's terminals, to stay off of some federal 'enemies list', I am beginning to consider self-censorship. I'm thinking maybe that Hitler did knock someone up, that the kid was raised by Richard Nixon, and that he is presently molesting us in our collective national shower.

It is all getting weird enough that I am going to get back to reading and writing science-fiction and history as a way to get out of this place. In the mean time, I am going to practice up on my 'Yes Sir's' in case my next book is slated to be confiscated by my Master's Loyal Slaves.

James LaFond, still lord of his used book bag, 6/9/2013

Jack-Boot Brigade #2

Gutting Fat Joe's House

© 2013 James LaFond

Fat Joe is in his early 40s. I run into him sometimes in the evening when he is headed back into town. Last night he was burdened with a stack of pizza boxes. Joe works just outside the city, and, on pay day, returns home to meet his grown children for a meal. You see, he lives in a 'bad' neighborhood where there is not a good pizzeria. Below is what he said last night, about two different kinds of heat.

"I am losing some weight with all of this heat, all kinds of heat. My children love cheese pizza, and you know, they have jobs of their own and buy me fish en chips en such, so I come with the pizza when it's my turn. I hope this is good pizza. It's nice to still be able to do with your family when they are all grown and moved…"

"...I am gutting the house. That is tough work in this heat. But I have to reorganize and make new—hidden—camera placements. The old placements will not due because they are known. I have had to move my collectables to storage. I believe though that the thieves will be back since I got them in trouble. They know about the cameras because one lost his job on it when I took the video to my lawyer.

"I live in a bad neighborhood—lots of drugs en crime. But it is my Mom's house. I'm not giving it up. I was proud of my collectables; mostly toys, but sports memorabilia as well; even had displays. None of those hoodlums in the neighborhood want toys; understand the value. Of course the sports memorabilia was stored out of view, and my signed documentation of authenticity and purchase were all well secured. My signature matches to that on the documents.

"Three times now the police have broken down my door, sayin' they was lookin' for drugs. Three times they stole my collectables—Transformers even! The one lost his job over it, and I have received the return of most of my collectables. It hurts though, that my collectables are targeted by thieves...You know they will be back. They don't let their own fall without payback. I'm working hard in this heat, gutting that old house and making concealable camera platforms. I will not be driven from my Mom's home..."

Dee, another passenger, spoke up, "It is not right to steal, not for anybody."

Fat Joe then relaxed a little more, as he is not tense in the first place, and smiled, "My, this pizza smells good, smells really cheesy. You all have a safe and blessed night and stay cool in this heat."

Welcome Aboard Mass Hysteria Transit

And Thank You For Leaving Your WMDs at Home

© 2013 James LaFond

Of the dozen or so law enforcement posters, stickers and statute plaques now plastered on MTA buses in the Baltimore area, this is my favorite. If I had not been under the Orwellian eye of the onboard camera system I would have pealed it off and slapped it on my machete fencing helmet. The entire decal is in the shape of a comic book speech bubble about the size of a volley ball.

IF YOU SEE SOMETHING, [in black]

SAY SOMETHING TM [in red]

REPORT UNATTENDED BAGS AND UNUSUAL BEHAVIOR [in black]

TO POLICE OR TRANSIT PERSONNEL [in black]

1-800-492-TIPS [in red]

SECURE TRANSIT.ORG [underlined]

UNITED WE STAND [in italic, imbedded in underline shading]

PURCHASED BY* FUNDS PROVIDED BY THE DEPARTMENT OF HOMELAND SECURITY.

The many examples of these print programing attempts in public spaces—along with the recently instituted messages in movie theaters to look to your left and right for suspicious persons—would seem overbearing, and perhaps frightening, if I noticed a single other person ever reading them. As it is the homeless people are rooting through their bags, the drug addicts are arranging drops with their drug dealers via Federal Flip Phones, and everyone else is glued to their flat crystal balls.

Actually the only thing troubling about these announcements is the easily generalized warning to report 'unusual behavior'. There should be reminders to report packages left behind—that was long overdue ten years ago. It just makes me feel uncomfortable as I am usually the only white person, and the only one reading a book. If anyone is going to look unusual on this bus it will be me.

Note the trademark notice after the initial slogan. That means someone is making a profit off of that rarified saying. I doubt if all the books I ever write will pull in that much dough.

-James, 7/30/13

*How about 'with'?

At Dusk

Jackboot Brigade #4

© 2014 James LaFond

I work at night in Baltimore County. For the last two months I have not spent an evening on the bus or on foot in Eastern Baltimore County without seeing a police officer questioning someone, either a pedestrian or motorist. The person being detained and questioned is rarely young, and never black. This runs to 16 episodes I have ticked off on my Everfresh pineapple juice receipt over the past 24 trips to work taken in that 60 day period.

The chopper is always in the sky.

Cops are always visible, never absent from my sight for more than 10 minutes as I walk.

Although I have walked this route for four years now, the cops still slow down and shadow me as I haul my old ass to work. I guess this is something like those hicks in Pennsylvania harassing that groundhog every February.

The store I work at is open 24 hours, so I see these cops come in to purchase their lunch. One of them says hello, the other five all glare at me, stand taller, and walk slower, in my presence. I guess that means I have 4 out of 5 readers out of that shift.

The past four nights I have worked I have noticed that at least one customer is pulled over and questioned on the parking lot.

One of the ladies I train lives in this same jurisdiction. She is very attractive and drives a nice car. She has told me that she is being pulled over by cops twice a week. When she asks 'why' they say it is because there have been getting complaints about her car driving through the neighborhood. She responds, "But I live here, how can I not drive through the neighborhood?"

These might just amount to typical cop dating attempts, taking into account her good looks.

I, personally, am glad that more motorists are being randomly targeted by police than pedestrians. I have a sense that these cops practiced on the likes of me so that they could harass the likes of you more efficiently.

Enjoy.

Now, I have long known that city cops pull over any lone young man who is not dressed like a hipster or yuppie, just on reflex. All of my black fighters and employees were routinely harassed by cops. At one point I had to schedule an extra man on my ghetto night crew to make up for the one who never made it to work because he got locked up for questioning the cops as to why he was being detained on his way to work. It must be tough being raised by women and thus being taught to backtalk on reflex.

There is a crime-fighting logic to this, because if you pull over five random young black guys you will bag someone with an outstanding warrant or who is in possession of something illegal, if just a joint or an open container. This insures corrections facilities will hit their occupancy targets, and also insures that every day guys will get the hardcore criminal abuse and training they need to come back out on the street as an effective criminal, necessitating more police overtime. Like I said, this makes sense on many levels.

Last night at work a customer, Nigel, a tall dignified looking white man of 55 years, walked into my section and began to speak to me. Something was bothering him. This is what he said.

"I'm stopping by after work out there to grab my groceries. I have no record. I have never done drugs. I only drink at home. I had it five under the limit. I have a new vehicle with no violations and my tags are recent. A young cop pulls me over, questions me, runs my I.D.

"I ask him what is wrong and he says that caravans are being stolen so they are pulling every caravan over. I say, 'If I was going to steal this thing I would not drive on the primary road where you are. If I was going to steal this thing I would be a young guy, not an old man on his way home from work.'

"He starts to get shitty and I tell him who my cousin is. He knows my cousin. He's a cop, in the same precinct. The kid then just salutes and says, 'have a good day sir'. I got the impression that even if I was stealing my own car, even if I was a young criminal, I could have just dropped my cop relative's name and I would have been passed through. Its feeling like we're behind enemy lines, like this is occupied territory.

"I know it's wrong to call a cop a pig, that it must hurt their feelings. I never thought I would get to this point, especially at my age. But fuck them, fuck them all! They are pigs. This is supposed to be a free country not a police state."

I don't understand what is behind this policing trend, or really even what it signifies. This conversation brought to mind the time I had lunch with a friend who had come down from New York. When he was going through his wallet he had a stack of dark cards. I asked him what they were and he explained [I forget the term] that they were a type of fraternal police card. If you have a friend in New York who is on the police force and belongs to a certain fraternal order, he can issue you a card dated for that year. He told me it was important to keep your issued cards together, so that you can prove to the cop who randomly pulls you over that you have maintained a lasting friendship with another police officer for the number of years indicated by your cards. Although it initially struck me as creepy and corrupt, upon reflection this sounds to me like a possible police union initiative to offer some comfort to people in a heavily policed city in which the chief executive demands stop and frisk tactics.

In the defense of the police, they are hired and trained to intimidate and suppress, not protect and serve. They are doing their job as dictated by the politicians you support. As a social trend marker I think there is something significant about the random stopping of apparently law-abiding middle-aged white men and women coming and going to work and to the supermarket, in an area where virtually all crime is committed by 15-25 year old unemployed black males. One might suspect that this has more to do with developing a cadre of police who will be able to implement an effective curfew system in the not too distant dystopia. It might just be related to the recent purchase of 200 infantry fighting vehicles by the Department of Homeland Security.

Over and out from the Peoples Republic of Maryland.

Harm City Hospital

Violence in the ER & the New Compliance Paradigm

© 2014 James LaFond

I train with a handful of staff members who work at three Baltimore Area hospitals, in the Emergency Room. Over the years I have been shocked at how much violence these people describe to me as happening in the Emergency Room and adjacent spaces. In the city it often has to do with gang members being shot and then relatives and set members coming in to demand life-saving measures, or rival gangsters coming in to finish the job.

In a New York City hospital a friend of mine works as an emergency room tech. He has to put up with much hysteria and occasional anger from bereaved family members. When I called to ask him for an out-of-town perspective on what these Baltimore area ER people had told me, he had this to say:

"We aren't supposed to do anything to protect coworkers, not even female staff. Security—your big wannabe guys—are there. If anything rough goes down they call the cops. The cops take no shit. The security though, they're selective. They jack up little old Chinese ladies that are worried about their husband all the time. But yesterday, this big black dude comes in and starts flexing, telling them he's gonna kick their F-n asses, and they back off, let him have the run of the place. I'm trying to communicate with the nurse on duty and she can't even think, she's so freaked out about this guy— and this guy is threatening me. But security—you know, with the bully mentality—they give him half the room. If we drew a line around the area they let this guy walk around in, he would be the emperor."

Harm City ER

Something quite different happened on this same weekend in Baltimore. Joey and Arty were working in the ER when 'this big muscled up drunk' just began throwing punches at Joey, who is a Wing Chun and jiu-jitsu novice. He simply protected himself against a series of 6 to 10 punches, and then clinched up and gently took down the much larger attacker. Joey and Arty held the man and calmed him until security and police got on the scene.

After security cuffed the man one of them picked him up in a chicken wing and slammed him to the floor for no apparent reason. The security and cops then took the man on a stretcher into another room. The man was heard pleading for mercy and complaining that his 'arm was breaking' as he was 'handled' 'behind a door'. Joey and Arty thought that all of the security and police actions were unnecessary and 'post-incident', in other words, 'payback'.

The Diminishing Art of Peacekeeping

I told them that two law enforcement people I spoke to recently have told me that three things are going into this increase in simple police overuse of force [and of course the imitation by security personnel who look up to the cops]:

1. the paramilitary 'homeland security' model of law enforcement that is coming down from the military contracting and SWAT community. I spoke to a recruiter for a military contractor based in Virginia this weekend, and he confirmed that local

police use their facility as their home training ground. Why are domestic cops training with military security personnel prepping for a tour in Chad or Afghanistan?

2. the DOJ injunction against submission holds which, according to an FBI supervisory agent I interviewed in 2001, 'has us going back to the stone age, beating people over the head'

3. prison overcrowding, which results in many 'pain-in-the-ass' offenders suffering little or no punishment as there is not enough room for more inmates. This later factor, I am told, contributes to a feeling among some officers that a little preliminary justice should be done in advance of booking.

Officers I have talked to go both ways on this. Some just admit to the fact that being in a decade long war with drug gangs has made them more aggressive and combative when it comes to 'peacekeeping' and 'pain-in-the-ass' work. One retired police lieutenant from a Baltimore area municipality had this to say:

"Most guys that you have to deal with are drunk. Let's face it barring the occasional irredeemable asshole, and the professional criminal, we are policing drunks. Now, down in the City, well, that is another thing; that is war brother. I feel for those City cops and will not judge them. I don't think I could have done twenty years of *that!* Fortunately, in an outlying area, you are doing more peacekeeping—but a lot of breaking and entering also. That calls for some diligence. Most of the drunks threaten you and want to struggle, and the next day, they apologize after they are sobered up. The lowlifes, the junkies and shoplifters and smash and grab punks, they just go limp and accept their fate. They'll be back out doing it again, regardless of their treatment.

"There is nothing to be gained from working these people over; no upside. But there is a downside. I've dealt with professional criminals. Those guys— most of them—have a code. We have our code. They have their code. If you understand their code—not saying you have to agree with it—you can grease the situation, avoid the violence. One time I was working with this—well, 'over eager' officer. He decides to knock this burglar around. Now, this guy did not resist. Had a record; definitely a pro. He was going in quiet, and my partner has to get in some licks. This guy is quiet, rangy, hard, has scars on his knuckles, has healed bullet wounds.

This dude has done at least twenty years on the street; a veteran with a code.

"He does not cuss, does not fight, does not make a peep; just gives the look, etching this idiot's face into his memory. When we put him away he gives a look of ice—locks eyes with the other cop—and says, "We'll meet again.""

"Now, how stupid do you have to be? Some guy that has been in the physical end of the criminal trade for decades, who is tough, who has beat down people and survived shootings, you're going to make an enemy out of this guy; make it personal?"

"The policeman's best friend is professionalism. You have to remember that one day you might be out with your lady, might be old and retired, and that guy—that ice man—might be there. Professionalism brother, it works wonders in many an occupation and is an absolute necessity for the peace officer, if a peace officer is what he desires to be."

You know what, if every cop was like that guy, I'd organize a fundraiser for the local precinct. But what do I see when I walk down to the local supermarket on Easter weekend? Two cops beating the shit out of an 18-year-old employee for spitting in the gutter on his coffee break. No arrest, no citation, nor record, just another cop hater, who could have been nicely told that spitting in public was not sanitary, and would, 'by the way Romeo, discourage the most desirable young ladies from associating with you.'

I'll do what I can to keep abreast of incidents from local hospitals, but will be mindful to obscure the hospital and the identity of the staff. Anything like this going down in a hospital has law suit written all over it. Hell, half the people who use the hospital ER for their medical care are already thinking law suit on their way in the door because people at their income level are targeted with TV ads by ambulance chasing lawyers.

Breaking Up The Pack

Harm County Police in Action

© 2014 James LaFond

Last Friday night I was taking my coffee break up front at about 1 in the morning when a Harm County cop walked in and asked if we were having any trouble with gangs of youths. [We may not refer to them as 'kids' as black mothers often regard this term as a slur in the Baltimore area and will file a slander suit against any proprietor who uses the term 'kid' to refer to her teenage shoplifter.]

We answered, "Not tonight," as there had been trouble earlier in the week with kids fighting, driving recklessly on the lot, and trying car doors. I stopped using my pen to take notes on the Seal Team Six book I was reading and did my best to record the cop's monologue.

"A party just let out down the street and we have a gang of kids. I didn't let them in the McDonalds and the drug store closed down. You cannot let them in here or they'll just spread out and smash and grab. Is this your only entrance and exit?"

"Yes Sir," said Bubba.

"I have backup coming. We'll have one on the lot and one here at the door. I'm not sure if they're from the neighborhood or from the city. If they're from the city it could get ugly. They go onto every lot and down every street and alley trying doors. Have they been bringing in change to cash in the machine?"

"Just the other night, three of them, a whole jug of change," answered Bubba.

"That's mostly from cars. We have officers out their trying to break them up now, the rest of us locking down businesses. The strategy is to break them into smaller groups otherwise they frenzy. If you need anything give me a call. I'll be out front."

Within five minutes he had made an arrest on the lot and the property was becoming a mobile field headquarters for processing hoodlums. By 3 in the morning we had a whole squad of cops on the property, a command center for combating our feminized youth.

Although, as a loner, I am routinely harassed by cops and can expect zero help from them, when I operated a business in Harm City, they were my cavalry. I could fight guys at the door, tackle them in the store and run interdiction for vulnerable customers on the lot—and sometimes even chase guys off the property. But I was one unarmed guy. To the extent that I was successful, I was only effective because the hoodlums knew that the cops would eventually get there, and that they would back me up.

In the city the swarming tactics were pioneered by younger teenage girls. In the county it is older teenage boys. My experiences living and working in Baltimore County and Baltimore City easily equate to military situations.

In the city running a retail outlet is analogous to running an embassy while the city is being overrun and infiltrated by the enemy. You don't get protection from the cops, but relief and counterstrikes.

In the county living in a home or running a business is like operating just across a demilitarized zone. County cops—particularly along bus lines and on the city line—swarm as aggressively as Africanized killer bees. In some cases they seek only to drive the crowds of hoodlums across the city line as there are too many to arrest.

For the most part I have been very impressed with the effectiveness of city and county cops when it comes to providing security for businesses. This makes sense from an organizational standpoint. Facility security is perfect for conventional police forces.

The differences are as follows:

1. City cops do nothing to protect homeowners, where county cops are as aggressive in their protection of residents as the city cops are of businesses. In the city homeowners and renters might as well be homesteaders.

2. County cops act as border guards where city cops exhibit no such priorities.

3. Since city cops are tasked with aggressively pursuing the Drug War* they prioritize the

targeting of lone males and generally ignore groups of males. It is therefore advantageous for unarmed and armed violent criminals to operate in packs, making the city far more dangerous to ordinary citizens. On the other hand, county cops go after packs of males and teens like blue blood cells bent on stopping an invader.

4. When a city cop responds to a call his time is usually not much worse than the county cop. His problem is lack of backup. For reasons I know nothing about city cops are alone on the scene five to ten minutes into a call, where county cops are at squad strength within five minutes.

*I am giving city cops a pass here, and assuming that this harassment of lone males and their ignoring of packs of violent youths and car loads of drive-up muggers, is a reflection of the Baltimore City Police Department's mission statement, which is certainly based on federal drug-arrest demands related to federal funding.

In any case, even though I think they exhibit questionable ethics for taking free drink and food from the convenience stores that are at their mercy, I must applaud the Baltimore County Cops of the three precincts I have lived and worked in, for operating effectively as a unit—and in quite a novel manner from a Harm City perspective—as aggressive protectors of the citizens and business owners as well.

'Rat-Smack City'

Breeders Digest #22

© 2014 James LaFond

The 'Can't Crack an Egg' Award of 2014 goes out to an example of one of the worst practitioners of ground-and-pound-while-bald-wannabe-MMA-California-cop-Fu in all of fistic history. An Officer of Cloven Hoof scored 10-15 rights hands on one crazy chick and could not even get her cuffed. The lady was walking on a freeway, which is against the law everywhere in the U.S. unless an alien invasion is in progress. So, she certainly deserved to be taken down and out. But dude, you can't whoop one girl's ass? And it's not like it was Rhonda I'm-afraid-to-misspell-her-last-name was your opponent. Let the hair grow or go down to Hunting Beach and talk to Tito about putting some guns in your ground game. This happened on Freeway 10 near La Brea Avenue. Please be compassionate and leave a pink boxing glove there in commemoration of Officer Limp Fist's manhood.

On the upside, Chicago kill shots are improving over last summer, with their boyz racking up 11 kills in 60 shootings. Another year of improvement like this and we should be able to stage a championship shoot out between the Baltimore Boyz and the Chicago Boyz. Perhaps we could use Toledo Ohio as a battleground?

You tree huggers will be glad to hear that we have been in a 10 year cooling cycle, with U.S. temps down 0.7 degrees. I am personally hoping for another ice age so that my Neanderthal genome can once again count for something other than sunburn. But with all of those earth mother rapists burning fossil fuels there might be a postponement of my knuckle-dragging landbridge reunion.

Heroin futures are up in the Panty Waist State my friends. Maryland is officially the most heroin addicted state of the Union with 10% of Marylanders doing the dope fiend lean! There is no way this could have anything to do with our five star welfare benefits package.

The rat Mecca of the U.S. is New York.

Second in rat population is Boston.

Third is Baltimore, and we aren't even half as big as one of Gotham's five boroughs. That makes Harm City the per-capita rat and smack capital of the United States of America.

I am headed over to the Harm City archive right now to update Rat Ratification and place it at the head of the main page. Look for it below this piece.

'The 13th Cop'

Notes on Body Language Cues

© 2014 James LaFond

Where I work, at Free Food For Fat F...s we are used to seeing cops, usually two at a time, coming through to buy their groceries while on duty, which is fine with us, as it sure beats getting robbed. Until last night here were a dozen cops from this Harm County precinct that I recognize on sight, none of whom I know by name.

Of these 12 4 have actively harassed me while walking to work or have violently glared at me as I go about my toil and they shop for groceries.

3 of these 12 law officers have been courteous and polite, as a knight should be when he passes by one of us serfs in the field who toil to feed his horse and fill the war chests of his master.

Of these 12 5 have never acknowledged my existence, which is how I like it.

Last night—this morning really—at 1:15 a.m. two very large cops were packing boxes full of doughnuts as I rotated the yogurt case. After my experience last Friday [I'll get to that] I now look over my shoulder at blue uniforms behind me. Until this past Friday, at the glimpse of a blue uniform, I would instinctually look to the floor like a peasant with downcast eyes before his lord unless I was caught unawares and accidentally made eye contact with a cop, which is slightly more likely to result in the cop becoming uncomfortable than it is for him to greet me cordially, by the 4 to 3 margin cited above.

As I broke down a Dannimals strawberry/kiwi box and glanced over my shoulder a second time at the 2 beefsters the larger older one, a man with light brown wavy hair who stood 6' 4", weighed about 260, had drooping man-breasts, and a heavy brow ridge glared at me harshly. Our eyes met and he went into stare down mode, straightening up his slouching shoulders, knitting his brows, clenching his jaw tightly, and squeezing his hands together into fists.

I immediately knew that I had slipped into my normal work posture, which is one of easy confidence, as I am a renowned expert at this lowly task. The body language is similar to a tennis pro serving, nonchalant and kind of arrogant. I normally, on sighting a cop, make a conscious decision to dump all surety, confidence and serenity out of my being, to roll my shoulders and lower my eyes before the might of my earthly lords—seriously, cops never hassle you when you adopt that kind of pathetic posture and sambo gait—but this guy just happened to lock eyes with me when I was calculating the time—which I do by comparing my breathing rate to my work rate. My timer is breaking down so I do it more often these days to stay within 5 minutes of true time.

If you want a cop to get aggressive you do one of three things: back talk him, run, or look him in the eye like you are an equal. I accidentally did the later and he started eye-fucking me; boring those eyes into me, perhaps trying to elicit a comment, perhaps unthinkingly expressing his need to dominate, just as I had unthinkingly forgotten to feign submission and had permitted him to see the real me, the me that feared his uniform and despised him. I don't suppose I was any more guiltless in this adolescent moment than he.

But someone needed to grow up in a hurry. I picked up the case of raspberry Dannimals and began freighting that while I checked the dates on the lid of the 32 once Dannon plain nonfat yogurt. I did not look up again until my master's loyal slave and his squire were on their way. I admonished myself for permitting myself to slip into a human moment during my brief time as a robot which provides me with writing and training freedoms I had previously only dreamed of before going into reverse retirement.

Besides, Officer Manbreast was just

Probably

Intuiting

Guilt

I have had this same stare down with many a red neck on county parking lots, many a violent black man on ghetto sidewalks. I knew immediately what this was. For some reason this guy did not think I feared him enough and wanted me to say something stupid that would justify his feeling of uneasiness—the thing about these types is they don't have a plan, but are impulsively violent. He is the 13th cop I can visually recall that I have had eye contact with on this job, and he is vastly insecure, and likes to hurt people. I know this with a certainty. His witless partner, the younger more fit version who has yet to earn his man boobs, was goo-gaaaing over the chocolate éclairs. This thug at least had the instinctual need to dominate and has surely been effective under pressure. I suppose he is what a certain number of his kind need to be.

Yes, last Friday night, I once again had my back to the shopping world. I have been attacked from behind twice by people while stocking shelves in food markets and have never entirely gotten comfortable with a lurker behind me. If the person is looking over my shoulders for more than say 10 seconds, I will turn and say, "Can I help you find something sir?"

As I did this I found that the customer behind me was a rather quiet cop, a cop with some sneak to him, not a clomping hard shooed batman utility belt jockey, but a tall muscular, athletic black dude in his early 30s.

He put his hands on his hips and said, "What's your name."

I immediately felt that sense of clarity when one knows if he says the wrong word, he is going to the floor. Obviously an employee, working away at cleaning the yogurt shelf, this cop decided I was a suspect! I answered "James. Can I help you find something?"

"No, I'm just looking for someone."

Then he was off into the stockroom. Moments later this cop and another NFL tight end sized human Doberman, but Caucasian, came out of the stockroom laughing and smiling. In their wake little Anthony, the 120 pound doughnut maker, staggered out onto the floor holding his heart and looking at me, "Jesus, I thought I was getting cuffed to a water pipe—what the hell! They just walked up on me."

Anthony and I both had the misfortune of wearing gray shirts on the night that some jerk in a gray shirt hit his girlfriend down the street from our job site—never mind that he was half my age and twice Anthony's size. I have fought since 1976 in various sports and in altercations, and have trained hundreds of fighters. I know when a guy is thirsting to beat some other guy down. I had just met him again.

This morning, on my way to the bus stop, as the sun rose over Eastern Baltimore County, a black man— a small heavyweight—walking the other way on the far side of the street seemed to recognize me, stopped, glared at me, and then began crossing the street to intercept me, putting his thick hotdog-fingered hands up in a combative posture. I switched my umbrella to the right hand, slid my right shoulder out from under the backpack strap so I could use it as a shield in my left hand, and lowered my gait but kept walking. He took one step into the gutter, registered my preparation with a time lag indicative of a drunk, and backed off, grunting to himself, "Uhugh, uhugh" and continuing on his way.

This is the problem with living in the middle of a world at war with itself. The same visual cues that keep that jerk from attacking me will send the cop after me like a heat-seeking missile—because the cop is conditioned to deal with that asshole. Imagine if I had maintained the cowering body language I adopted at 4 a.m. to keep the third pair of cops to shop the doughnut section from getting edgy with me? That would have encouraged this guy.

The rest of the way home I engaged in some self-examination, paid more attention than usual to how other bus patrons regarded me, and came to the conclusion that I have been too deep in thought considering how best to archive my online writing into a POD format, and have been guilty of wearing a single face; have been letting the world see me for what I am instead of what it needs me to be.

I have given up on most of the things people strive for. But I currently have 6 years worth of work ahead of me to complete the books I have outlined, and would like to make it to 58. If I'm going to pull that off I've got to have at least three phony faces on hand at all times or I'll end up under some younger man's shoes.

Afterward

I believe that Narco Night Train is the last of my thematic Harm City books. The Narco State is where this has all been headed since before I started documenting it in 1996, and it is here to stay. Beginning in December 2015 I intend to publish a single annual Harm City Reader.

Let's hope you don't make it between the pages of that.

May you live quietly free and find your peace of mind on some seldom-travelled road.

James LaFond, Thursday, 10/30/2014